TRIBAL CONTEMPORARY ISSUES
Appraisal and Intervention

About the Author

Ramnika Gupta, former member of Bihar Vidhan Sabha, is presently President of Ramnika Foundation. Also, she is editor of a Hindi quarterly journal *Yudha Rat Aam Aadmi,* and Joint Secretary of Democratic Writers Association (Bihar-Jharkhand Chapter) as well as Member of National Council of Democratic Writers Association. She is a well-known Hindi poetess and novelist and has to her credit many collections of poems, short stories, novels and essays. She has bagged several awards for her literary achievements and social service.

About the Translator

Presently Reader and Head, University School of Humanities and Social Sciences, GGS IP University, Delhi, Dr. Anup Baniwal has been teaching English and Communication Skills to both Undergraduate and Post graduate students for the last 18 years. His areas of academic and research interest include Indian English Fiction on Partition, Indian Writing in English Translation, Translation and Communication Skills. Apart from authoring a book entitled *Representing Partition: History, Violence and Narration,* he has also regularly contributed research and review articles in various journals, newspapers and magazines.

About the Foundation

Ramnika Foundation, a non-political, non-commercial and absolutely secular organisation, works for bringing an equalitarian change in society through empowering the marginalised and oppressed communities like the tribals, dalits, minorities and women. Working in the social sector for the last many years, the Foundation has the distinction of piloting and pioneering many successful initiatives, both at the ideological and material levels.

The Foundation embodies efforts and struggles, hopes and aspirations of the common people for developing a dynamic and responsive civil society, a society which ensures human rights and dignity, health and education to the marginalised millions.

TRIBAL CONTEMPORARY ISSUES

Appraisal and Intervention

Ramnika Gupta

Translator
Anup Beniwal

Published for
Ramnika Foundation
by
CONCEPT PUBLISHING COMPANY, NEW DELHI-110 059

Cataloging in Publication Data—DK
Courtesy: D.K. Agencies (P) Ltd. <docinfo@dkagencies.com>

Guptā, Ramaṇikā, 1930-
Tribal contemporary issues : appraisal and intervention / Ramnika gupta ; translator, Anup Beniwal.
p. cm.
Translated from Hindi.
In Indian context.
Includes bibliographical references.
Includes index.
ISBN 13: 9788180694752
ISBN 10: 8180694755

1. Adivasis—India—Politics and government. 2. Adivasis—India—Social conditions. 3. Tribes—India —Social conditions. 4. Adivasis—India—Economic conditions. 5. Tribes—India—Economic conditions. 6. Rural women—India. I. Beniwal, Anup, 1962- II. Title.

DDC 305.800 954 22

ISBN -13 : 978-81-8069-475-2
ISBN -10 : 81-8069-475-5

First Published 2007

Published and Printed by
Ashok Kumar Mittal
Concept Publishing Company
A/15-16, Commercial Block, Mohan Garden
New Delhi (INDIA)

Phones : 25351460, 25351794
Fax : 091-11-25357103
Email : publishing@conceptpub.com

Preface

Adivasi issues are drawing attention for some time now. I raised these issues in 1998 through 'Yudharat Aam Aadami', a magazine published by Ramnika Foundation. Two special issues of the magazine were devoted to Adivasi literature in which works of more than 100 Adivasi writers were given place. This was the time when Akhil Bharatiya Adivasi Sahityik Manch was established.

In fact, in 2002, Ramnika Foundation, in association with Sahitya Akademy, organized India's first Adivasi Sahitya Sammelan, in which Adivasi writers from nine states participated. I have been writing on these issues regularly. My articles have been published in newspapers like Janasatta, Rashtriya Sahara, Hindustan, Prabhat Khabar, Ranchi Express and Aaj. My essays, highlighting the problems of Adivasis have also been published in several magazines, including Aravali Udghosh, Udbhavana, Swadhinta and Yudharat Aam Aadami. Akhil Bharatiya Adivasi Sahityik Manch, a sister organization of Ramnika Foundation, has organized several seminars in which Adivasi perspectives and points of view were voiced.

For the last 40 years, I have been living among the tribals, working for their welfare. I am trying to make aware the government and the people about the problems of Adivasis, in order to bring an attitudinal change towards the tribal community. Adivasis have their own history, culture, languages, and democratic social system. Equality, brotherhood and freedom are part of their lifestyle, and cooperation their habit. They have a long tradition of secularism—they respect the religion of others and do not thrust their beliefs on others. Love for nature is the way of their living. But unfortunately, the so-called main-streamists of India have made them to shut up. They are termed as uncivilized and their contribution to Indian history is negated.

They have their own language, and their literature is written in ninety languages. They have their own identity. But today, their very identity, language and culture are at the margin of their survival.

This year we are celebrating 150th year of first struggle of India's independence. But we are not ready to accept Adivasi's struggles for freedom. Even before 1857, the Pahariya Adivasis, under the leadership of Ramana Alhari, waged war against the British rulers. In 1922, Sriram Raju of Andhra Pradesh fought a battle against the British. But there is not a mention of it—neither in history nor in school curriculum. What we teach in schools is that Bhils are a tribal community and their primary occupation is thiefing. What a disgrace!

They have denied access to the forests. Efforts are made to snatch away their land, language and even their identity. In the name of development, they are compelled to migrate. They are made outsiders even in their own country.

But today, they have started voicing their concerns. Earlier, they used to speak what they were told to speak. Now, they themselves think about their problems. Ramnika Foundation is making all efforts in giving voice to them. I have also raised these issues in my essays, but in Hindi. Now these essays are going to be published in English. In these essays, I have tried to present the aspirations of Adivasis as well as the meaning of freedom, from their own point of view.

I have been living among the Adivasis for the last 40 years. I have run several movements for them. I have felt the change taking place among them. They want to live and develop, but in their own style. They want freedom to take their own decisions. They want equality. They are the oldest democratic groups of the world. They have taught democracy to the developed and developing countries of the world. The Western society has accepted their thought, but negates their presence. Today, their survival is in danger. This is our duty to help them survive with self-respect and dignity. This book is an effort in this direction. Many of my essays could not find place in this book, as they are not translated because of time shortage. Wait—they will be brought out very shortly.

Ramnika Gupta

Translator's Note

It is a delight to go through Ramnika Gupta's original work in Hindi. Her concerns, invariably activist and interventionist in scope, are people oriented. Straddling across genres—poetry, short stories, biography, prose essays, criticism, and journalism—her creative and critical corpus evolves around the socio-political, economic and existential plight of people at the margins—Adivases, *dalits*, and women. Even among them, she is particularly concerned with *yudhrat aam adami*, the common people—workers in mines, domestic and industrial labour, dislocated tribals, disadvantaged women—who are consciously and actively engaged in struggles that don't stop at mere survival but go far beyond to achieve one's rightful place/space in the socio-economic and political scheme of things.

Ramnika Gupta may not share the same location, but she, as a co-participant in the plight of people and as an involved activist, understands and empathizes with them. Her advocacy of their concerns is genuine, not patronizing. And it shows in her creative and critical writings. There is a kind of hard-hitting frankness and sincerity about whatever she does or writes about. Instead of engaging the readers in the flourish of language, she has the habit of engaging them directly with the topic at hand. This habit of calling a spade a spade and the attendant sincerity of purpose is not a mere posturing, intellectual fad or a political/marketing gimmick with her, it springs from a sense of commitment that is attendant on an excruciating process of negating the self by putting it on public display, not as a self-aggrandizing spectacle but as a text that reflects the mechanization of the colonial-patriarchal society on its subject. Her autobiographical sketches are a testimony to this. Her long career as a trade union activist further reiterates this fact.

This quality of negating the self and being one with the disadvantaged 'other(s)' is indeed remarkable, given the reality of Indian context. Within the conservative milieu, with its more often than not hypocritical ethos, an outspoken and an outgoing woman is always faced with derogatory insinuations. In fact, it is one of the hardest challenges a woman activist still faces in India. An average woman may find herself dissipated at this initial stage itself. It is rare, if one doesn't take up the easier options offered by 'sponsored' NGOs now-a-days, for a woman to overcome this initial hurdle dispassionately and tread the un-trodden paths that demand immediate and utmost attention and priority. Ramnika Gupta is aware of this onerous task and commitment that it demands, especially from women, when she says: "From us, who talk of equality and seek job parity, this issue demands a commitment: let us shed our 'touch-me-not' image, and as competent women, adapt ourselves for every task and make ourselves capable of taking risks. And I can say this on the basis of my own experiences that this 'touch-me-not-complex' is typically middle class syndrome." Raminka Gupta does not only lead by example, but also, in the process, raises many pertinent questions with regard to our priorities as responsible citizens, and also our methodologies for social intervention. She is not an armchair 'revolutionary', neither is activism social luxury for her.

Her activist writings are a treasure trove of information. She believes in extensive documentation of issues, facts and data to delineate and substantiate her concerns. These facts have been gleaned from her first hand experiences and encounters as a trade union leader and a politician, her engagement and involvement as a fellow writer, translator and commentator on *dalit* and *adivasi* writing, its texts and contexts, and an extensive study of the published material. Most of the essays in this book are an outcome of her engagement with these issues as an editor of *Yudhrat Aam Adami*, both as peoples' movement and a journal (in Hindi) that documents Ambedkrite, Indigenous and Peoples' literature. These essays also reflect the focus of her eponymous foundation.

A well-known figure in Hindi belt, it is high time her works were also introduced to the wider world. This objective and need informs this translation. The need to shake off the complacency of the English speaking middle class elite—the bedrock of LPG forces that threaten to further marginalize the already marginalized—and to sensitise them to the reality of the marginalized masses and their problems is an express purpose of this translation.

In the essays included in this anthology Ramnika Gupta's socially oriented reflections are generally underlined by a threefold purpose: construction, critique and conditioning. She critiques the ignorance of the mainstream classes and the indifference of the mainstream power clique to the condition of the margins. She constructs or showcases the world-view, aspirations and inspirations of the margins so as to inform and expand the horizons of her prospective readers. In other words, having jolted them out of their smugness and privileged but narrow locations, Ramnika Gupta's writings condition her prospective readers to empathizely connect with and enter into the life world and mindset of the margins. That this conditioning is affected for a particular purpose and from a particular ideological location comes across loud and clear in her writings; it is not present in her writing as a hidden agenda. It makes her writings transparent and purposeful, even prophetic. If the plight of the people present in her writings is not heeded to, if the mainstream keeps appropriating or hegemonising their culture and life mores or if it fails to safeguard their political and social interest and aspirations, or if it keeps on exploiting them unabated for its own vested interests; the consequences can be fatal for the multicultural fabric of India as a nation. The repetitive and often rhetorical loudness in Ramnika Gupta's prose, if seen in this context, comes out as a well thought out strategy on her part to catch hold of the smug reader by the collar and drill into his/her consciousness a worldview he/she is perilously ignorant of.

Her essays have been an eye opener for me and I hope that this translation will go a long way to illuminate the consciousness of many more.

Anup Beniwal
Professor

New Delhi

Contents

1

Adivasis

The Precursors of the Freedom Struggle of 1857

150th anniversary of 1857 or the First War of India's Independence is being celebrated this year. As documented in history, it was a time when the Indian Raja's, feudal lords and *nawabs* took upon themselves to drive away the British from India. It is true that the people of the country sided and cooperated with the Raja's in this struggle. The historians have however failed to document one of the most significant facts of this history, viz., the participation and contribution of the indigenous people/*Adivasis* in this struggle. *Adivasis* were in fact the precursors or initiators of the armed rebellion against the British, but historians have conveniently ignored this fact. In fact, just a year ago, in 2005, we celebrated the 150th anniversary of Sido Kanhu's call to *Santal Hool,* in Jharkhand.

Adivasi-warriors never turned away from the battlefield, they fought to the end. A dead leader would be immediately replaced by another so as to lead one's contingent. Considering that they were no monarchs but ordinary people, this was a singularly remarkable feat. Their leadership was not hereditary; each one was a potential leader.

Today let's salute the heroes of that freedom struggle and recall those *Adivasi*-warriors from north-east to extreme south-west, who either took part in the war of 1857 or who, in their unique ways, continued to resist the British before the war in 1857 or long after it was over, died fighting, accepted the noose without yielding—and did not side with the British out of avarice.

Even before 1857 the *Adivasi*-communities had, at their own levels, engaged the British in many amazing battles throughout India so as to dissuade them from settling down (in India). For three-quarters of a century, starting at the end of 18th century, *Adivasis* continued to harass the British. The entire Khandesh, an *Adivasi*-majority region that nestles in the lap of Satpuras, had turned against the British in 1825. The British could not bring peace to the region despite the power of their money (in the form of wages) or munitions. *Adivasi* battles continued into the 20th century.

This chain of tribal rebellions has a past that precedes 1857 by many years. It all began in 1766, ninety years before 1857, in Nala, Jamtara and Kundahint in Jharkhand where the rebellion against the British had erupted under the leadership of Ramna Alhari (Paharia). This came to be known as *Paharia* revolt. It continued till 1778. Tracing the history of tribal revolts, Manmohan Pargi adds: "The *Adivasis* of Pune-Nasik region in Maharashtra also share the honour of rising in struggle against the British."

Following Paharia resistance, Rani Shaveshwari raised the banner of revolt in 1781. Baba Tilka Majhi raised a battalion of, soldiers, and raiding Bhagalpur in the first week of 1784, took many adjoining areas under his control. He also fought many battles in the region of Munger and Santal *parganas*. Baba Tilka had arrowed to death. Augustus Cleavland, the Commissioner of Bhagalpur, when he saw him molesting an *Adivasi* girl. Tightly securing his hands and feet with ropes, the English fastened Tilka Majhi to four horses and dragged him all the way from Sultanpur to Bhagalpur. Even then Tilka Majhi did not die. He was ultimately hanged on a Tree at the Bhagalpur Square.

Vishnu Maanki led the *Bundu* revolt against the British from 1797 to 1798, and Dhukkhan Maanki kept alive the sparks of this rebellion in Tamar from 1800 to 1808 till it virtually turned into a conflagration. This *Munda* revolt of Tamar continued unabated during 1819-20. During the same period, Rugdev and Konta Munda triggered the *Kol* revolt, and *Ho* revolt also happened the same year; the fire of revolts thus engulfed the British in Jharkhand. In the *Kol* revolt of 1828-1832, under the leadership of Bindrai and Singhrai, the *Kol* rebels took control of the king's palace. The *Adivasis* had thus succeeded in forming an independent government well before 1857.

In 1854-56, the kettledrums for the great *Santal Hool* were struck under the leadership of the four Murmu brothers, Sido, Kanho, Chand and Bhairo. It shook the foundations of the foreign empire. The *Santal Hool* had begun on the night of June 30, 1856 with the slogans—*Hool bahar jitkaar, Hool hegal jitkaar*. More than ten thousand *Adivasis* were killed in this uprising. Sido and Kanho were hanged, Chand and Bhairo died fighting. In this uprising masses joined hands with the revolutionaries by contributing clothes, shoes, *laathis*, pots and pans for drinking water etc., for the cause.

Post 1857, Birsa Munda's great uprising, *Ulgulaan* continued unabated from 1895 to 1900. Birsa had envisioned this struggle as an emancipatory class struggle for the destruction of British revenue system and feudal-contractor-moneylender nexus. Its aim was to reclaim tribal rights over forest and land, and to protect *Adivasi* identity, autonomy and culture. It was, in fact a revolution against the British.

1902 *Santal* uprising was their last battle. Meanwhile *Kharwars, Majhies, Korwas, Kharias, Gonds* and *Mundas* continued with their many rebellions.

While these revolts were unfolding in Jharkhand, various other revolts surfaced elsewhere in the country.

In Bastar, the *Bhil* revolt against the British was simply amazing. According to Manmohan Paargi in his essay published in Special Issue of *Yudhrat Aam Aadmi—Adivasi Swar Aur Nai Shatabdi* Part-II—"More than one lac *Adivasi*-revolutionaries confronted the army of colonel Gamer. The *Adivasi* heroes were cordoned by deceit, and gunned down. The remaining rebels were rounded up and were hanged from trees at the *sadar bazaar* of Jagdalpur." In Madhaya Pradesh, the *Raja Muria* tribals of *Angarwara Paragna* rose in revolt in which the people of *Bhatra* and *Mahra* communities had also participated.

India celebrates its Republic Day on 26th January, and its Independence Day on 15th August. But no one celebrates the birth and death anniversaries of brave Sangoli Rayanna whose birth and death incidentally coincides with these dates.

Rani Chinemma, the queen of Kittur, after the death of her husband, had entered into a conflict with the British for safeguarding the rights of her adopted son. She was childless. She was imprisoned. This was the first battle against the British in Karnataka. Rani Chinemma was born 33 years before the famous queen of Jhansi. Rayanna was the revenue-collector of the British. After the queen was taken into custody, he took charge of the revolt and did not let the battle of Kittur slacken. Rayanna organized similarly inclined people throughout the state and carried on with the battle. On 26th January 1933, Rayanna was executed by hanging in Nandgaon. He kissed the noose singing songs of his motherland. The heroic martyrdom of brave Sangoli Rayanna, who was born on 15th August 1794, in the Dhanagar family of Sangoli, in Belgaum district, is unique in the history of Karnataka in India.

From the beginning of 19th century till 1857, for fifty years till the first war of independence, East India Company had to face stiff resistance in the Northeast from *Lushai, Singdoh, Jaintia* and *Kachhari* communities under the leadership of Maniram Barua, Tirot Singh, Tikendrajit Singh, U. Kiang Nangbah and Ropuiliani, among others. For forty years, *i.e.*, from 1858 to 1898, the duration that the British administration took to consolidate its hold on the entire Northeast, the people of the region did not let them enjoy peace.

By 1774 the Jaintia king had fought a war with Major Hoenikker that continued till 1821. On 4th April 1829, Tirot Singh attacked the British. He spearheaded a massacre of an entire British post. This started the battle which dragged on for many years. The revolt continued for three years and he was put under house arrest for life. Though many of these people were sacrificed, but they too gave the British a tough fight.

Nangbah, a commoner had closely watched Tirot Singh battling the British. In fact Britisher's prevented Khasis to burry their dead one on the prescribed *Shamshan Ghat* (Cemetery). They also put a ban on the prevelent custom of bringing weapons in the festivals. This agitated Khasis. They were very much annoyed with these foriegn rulars because of their interference in their religious matters, customs and lifestyle. Imposition of tax by Britishers on Khasis further deteriorated the situation and the war started. Many platoons of the British army were deployed to capture Nangbah. He was caught by deceit and was hanged from a tree in front of a crowd that ran into thousands. Before stepping on to the noose, he is believed to have told his tearful country-folks: 'If my face turns towards left as they pull the rope, it would mean that you would get independence within 100 years, but if it turns right, you will be slaves for ever.' The freedom came in 1947, well within hundred years. His martyrdom is commemorated even today.

After the death of her husband Vaandula, queen Ropuiliani blew the trumpet of revolt in Mizoram. Though her sons were killed in the battle, she did not yield. She proclaimed that she would drive the English away from Mizoram and would not let her people work like slaves. For the British, she was a born rebel. She was arrested in 1893 and died in jail on January 3, 1895.

Nagaland, Mizoram and Assam in the Northeast are witness to amazing tales of heroism. It is a testimony to their organizational-prowess and skills that the *Adivasis* of Nagaland managed to attack the British for nineteen years. According to Manmohan Pargi, "282 British officers and soldiers were killed in these attacks. *Nagas* withstood the might of the British army equipped with modern armaments for five months."

On the other side in Rajasthan, while the royalty and the elites were busy playing host to the British, *Adivasis* were challenging the British through their folk songs:–

O white man, why have you
Come to our land;
Go back to your country?

(*Yudhrat Aam Adṃi*, Special Issue, Part-1)

The name of Khajya Nayak of Madhya Pradesh would top the list in any discussion on *Adivasi*-battles against the British in 1857. In Khandesh, *Adivasis* kept on fighting the English from 1818 to 1850. Despite their superior arms and army the British could not decimate these *Adivasis*. Khajya Nayak was among those heroes who had offered a formidable challenge to the British in 1857. He kept on fighting the English even after 1857. The fact whether he was betrayed or killed by deceit still continues to be debated, but one thing is certain, despite the assurance of clemency, Khajya did not surrender to the British.

Bhima Nayak and Mobasa Nayak were Khajya's friends. No body knows for certain the antecedents of Bhima Nayak, but he fought the English for ten years. With the death of queen of Jhansi, the revolt of 1857 came to an end in north India. Having reached Narmada, Tantiya Tope too turned back. But both Khajya and Bhima persisted with the battle.

Even when the war of 1857 was over, they continued fighting the British in the region of Nivaad, Khandesh and Nasik till 1867. His country's independence was the proclaimed aim of Bhima's exploits. He was arrested in 1867 and exiled from India.

Tantya Bheel comonly known as Tantya Mama was yet another notable revolutionary who was dreaded by the British administration. He was born in Nimad in Madhya Pradesh. The frenzy of the vindictive violence unleashed by the British, in the aftermath of revolution of 1857, had struck terror in the hearts of people. It was at this juncture that Tantya, a *Bhil*, confronted the English. Two of his associates, Dipya and Bijhnia, were arrested in 1880. Dipya escaped and rejoined Tantya, but Bijhania was hanged to death. There is a famous anecdote about Tantya. The English officer who had come to arrest Tantya happened to be one whom Tantya had escorted home as his luggage carrier. Tantya, a man with steel in his blood, confronted the officer: 'Sahib, I am Tantya, Won't you arrest me?' Hearing this officer was convulsed with terror and he returned to England in fright. Tantya was betrayed by his own *dharma bahnoi*, the husband of his *dharma* or *rakhee* sister on the day he had called on her for *rakhee*.

It was during the struggle of 1857 when *Komurams* fought the British for days and nights under the leadership of Ramji. Ramji Gond was arrested and was hanged near Nirmal to death by a tree. The tree is still known as the Ramji Chettu.

The Kuruchia *Adivasis* of Kerala too fought the British army to the last drop of their blood. Talakkar Chandu was their leader. This brave man kept fighting a British contingent of hundred soldiers till he was fully exhausted. Talakkar Chandu and Nilli, an *Adivasi* woman were the folk leaders of this movement. Nilli had also raised a separate army of women. Talakkar Chandu was caught and hanged to death.

In the second half of 19th century Govind Guru, besides leading *Adivasi* movements not only against English rule, but also against native kings and the *Begari* (forcing village workers to work without wages) practices of *jagirdars*, had spearheaded social reform movements. Apart from launching anti-liquor and pro-female education movements, he also fought against prevalent social evils and violence. He was born in a *Banjara* family. He established *sanmap sabhas* among *Bhil* and *Garasia* tribes. On the complaint of the native Rajput Raja's, the British raided his *dhuni* and massacred 1500 *Bhils* overnight. This massacre was bigger in scale than that of Jallianawala Bagh. This incident took place in Banswara located in Maangarh. Some times in 1880-81. He was imprisoned.

The last armoured battle was probably fought in 1922 under the leadership of Allari Sitaram Raju. His first encounter took place with Trem Nahity. On 25th December 1922 in Damanopalli, Raju and his comrades surrounded the English and killed their officers. Their rebellion is termed as 'Fituri' (a derogatory word) by the English. Sri Ram Raju had avowed that he would drive out the British from the country within a year. He ransacked three *thanas* (police posts) on August 22-23, 1922 and launched an anti-*lagan* (revenue), anti-liquor and pro-*panchayati raj* movement that continued for two years.

There are countless tales of revolt and heroism. Today we salute all these *Adivasi* warriors who participated in the struggle of 1857. We also salute those who ignited the spark of rebellion before 1857, transformed it into a conflagration, and did not let this blaze extinguish even after 1857.

2

Adivasi Writing

An Emerging Consciousness

Whereas on the one hand the *Adivasi* creative consciousness inheres in the self-articulation of its pains and in finding its own solutions, on the other it also embeds an awareness of the conspiracy by which the established canon has tried to keep tribal people outside the ambit of civilization. The following extract from Vahru Sonvane's poem 'Stage' provides us with an apt and accurate portrayal of the emerging contours of *Adivasi* creative consciousness. In this poem the *Adivasi* poet has etched out those feelings which not only shaped but also helped give vent to his creativity. While defining the emerging-consciousness in *Adivasi* writing, the poem also underlines the need for such writing, thus–

> We did not go up the stage
> That was made in our name
> Nor were we invited on to it
> We were shown
> Our place
> With pointed finger
> And we sat there (obediently)
> We were highly appreciated
> And 'they,' standing on the stage
> Kept telling us of our own misery
> "But our misery remained ours alone
> it was never theirs"
> We mumbled—uttered our doubts

"They" listened intently
And roared...
Pulling us by the ear admonished us
"Say sorry... otherwise..."

Along with a creative re-appropriation and self-presentation of one's pain, it is a consciousness that, piercing the age old silence, seeks to shatter the conventional canonical enclosures and Luxman Rakhas that have been drawn by the dominant. This consciousness inspired them to know their own culture, language, history, geography. They also became aware and wanted to know and investigate everything so that they can expose themselves and their culture to the outside world and say proudly—"Look! As a society our values have neither decayed nor any deformity has seeped into these—We have been living as a community—as a social group or collectivity—we have also been trying to forget the hardships inflicted on us by you by singing and dancing. You shoved us away from civilization—displaced us. We kept intact the mutual dialogue alive through flute and kettledrums. Now this dialogue has erupted as *Naada*—and the flute has become a 'flame'. Transcending the limits of language and race we have united with a resolve to enlighten the whole society. Our languages are now armed with pen. We have begun writing. We have become aware of our Identity also. Don't mislead us by calling us *'Banwasi's'* or forest-dwellers! We, the primordial inhabitants of earth, were born with nature, grew up and evolved with it. We are the ones who as co-participants and co-contributors believe in conserving nature. We don't want to dominate or rule it. We believe in co-existence—not in annihilation. We draw subsistence from nature and return back the same to her. We have begun writing now—against our forced dislocation caused by you. We won't let our identity, our self-pride and self-respect be destroyed. Living with our distinctive life-mores we would scale the ladder of change in a manner that would equip us to compete with you as equals—we have accepted the challenge to keep pace with civilization while keeping intact our individuality—our simplicity—and our collective identity—we will have to wrest-back our land—our forests from you—we shall learn in our mother tongue so that we, the native habitants, may unite. We shall discover our history. Haven't you progressed through our martyrdom and our decimation? We will bring this fact/truth to light and shall prove that we were saviors and protectors, not Rakashas, *i.e.* Damons. We were benevolent—not monsters. The king Mahabali who donated his whole kingdom to disguised Bawan was our ancestor. We never disguise to deceive."

Since *Adivasi* writers have scripted the truth of their lives—and have documented their life problems, theirs is a literature of life and not an imaginary tale for entertainment. The have also written about Birsa's *Ulgullan, Santal-Kol* uprising, and the execution of Sido Kanhu. Equipped with the *Adivasi*-consciousness, Bhujang Mesram, a poet from Maharashtra, wrote:

Birsa! you have to arrive from anywhere
Either on sickle that cuts grass
Or on an Axe that cuts the wood
From here or from there
From East-West or North-South
Turning into the breez of the farm
Come from anywhere
O My Birsa! people wait for you.

This consciousness imbued them with a sense of freedom, and made them aware of their might/strength (hidden in the clasp of their fist):

After years the news has broken in the Jungle
A moment ago came across a *baya;* (bird)
that told of weaving a nest
Like the one built five thousand years ago
Just keep on singing
The songs of liberation.
Hidden in the fist of Jungle
Is an invaluable story (of struggle)

Infused by the self-confidence inherent in this literary awareness or consciousness Mahadev Toppo exhorted thus:

He would pick up the bow
And
To preserve the green of the forest; the poet of the Jungle
Would beat the drum and blow the flute
Mounting his pen on the bowstring

For Grace Kujur the pen is mightier than the gun:

What would their guns and bullets accomplish?
Crossing the threshold thousand stories are there
Every nerve, is turning into bow
Just wait for the pen turning into an arrow.

An *Adivasi,* when mute, used his arrow to fight injustice. Now he is aware of the fatal potency of the pen and is eagerly looking forward to forge his creative prowess into a weapon, an arrow.

Tribal women too did not lag behind. Whenever she rummages through her history, she comes across a brave female soldier Sinagi Dai, holding on her own, alone in the battlefield against the Mughals. And in appreciation Grace Kujur vents forth:

This time, if your fingers tremble
Take note
I'll once again become 'Singi Dai'

Recollecting the times when they would march forth at *jani-shikar* to vanquish the enemy, she exhorts every *Adivasi*-woman, thus:

Jharkhand truly needs
A formidable *janishikar* once again.

A tribal is gradually becoming aware of the conspiracy to dislocate and distance him from the mainstream/civilization, and is quick to alert his community about it. Hariram Meena in his poem includes even the aboriginals of Andaman & Nicobar. He is worried about their fast dwindling race. He protests their expulsion from their land, thus:

> How would you prove,
> In the court of this civilization
> That this 'bhom' (land) was yours?

Watching the forcible eviction of his people from their land, the poet is agitated by their helplessness, and interrogates them:

> Behold!
> They are coming
> Your nerves are taut
> Your muscles are flexing
> Your bows and arrows ready
> You are united and one
> Yet do nothing
> You can strike back
> But are afraid
> Why—but why?

Indigenous writers want to reform their community, so that empowered it can stand eye to eye with the mainstream.

Nirmala Putul strikes hard at the dead traditions and malpractices prevalent in her own community, when she says:

> Oh just stop that
> Don't utter a word, Sajoni Kisku
> I remember when you, in your village Baagjori
> Had tilled the land
> The throne of *deotas*
> That dwell in *Majhi Thaan* of our hamlet was shaken
> The turban of honour of that empty-headed *Hadaam*
> The hereditary chief, tumble down and was defiled
> Then, harnessing you to the yolk

They had ploughed the field.
The monsters
Had made you eat fodder
Tethering you by the peg.

She cautions Chudka Soren:

What quantity of liquor your father had consumed
I am not sure
But the liquor consumed him.

She cautions Chudka about the plain-dwellers, who lure away *Adivasi* girls:

What jungle-beast was it Chudka Soren
That fled away with your sister Mungli, who
Had gone to gather fire-wood in the jungle.

In Rajasthan, *Adivasi* writers, through their research and writing, have been able to resurrect the revolt of Gobind Guru and the martyrdom of Kalibai. Ramesh Chandra Vadera and Khemraj Pargi have traced the history of Gobind Guru and Kalibai through folk songs. Hariram Meena has also explored this theme in his article. Today we know that a massacre bigger in scale than that at Jalianwala had taken place at Maangarh, where the English, in connivance with Rajput chieftains of Rajasthan and Gujarat, had shot dead 1500 Adivasis in a single night in the hills of Maangarh. But this incident remained buried in history. It is only now that it is being documented.

The movement that Gobind Guru, a staunch advocate of education, had spearheaded for establishing of schools for boys and girls, for non-payment of taxes to the government and interest to moneylenders, was kept alive by people in their folk songs and folktales; now these are being penned on paper and sculpted in stone by the *Adivasi* artists.

The following song by Gobind Guru that reverberates through the nooks and corners of Rajasthan turned out to be a prophecy for freedom:

O Buratia I refuse to acquiesce
My writ runs in Delhi
In Ahmedabad my *jajam* (seat)
My armies in Jaambu
In Maangarh my *dhuni* (base)
I recognize him as the chief
Who proclaims
The authority of Gobind Guru
White man I won't acquiesce...

(*Buratia stands of British white man*)

Adivasi writers have also tried to unearth the sources of their languages. Moraji Devgam has discovered *Mundari* words in the languages of Zambia, Mongolia, Nigeria and Germany. He has even prepared a script for *Ho* language. It is a manifestation of the energy and awareness of *Adivasi* writers that they have been making utmost efforts to develop their languages. *Santali* speakers have invented a script called *Olchiki*. This script is even being taught in West Bengal. They are now trying to demonstrate that the *Mundari* language and its '*dupub*' (root) culture has been the harbinger of universal human society. The search is on for *Mundari* and *Kudux* words even in Vedas.

Pitching for his mother tongue, Pushp Pushakar suggests links among *Mundari, Khadia, Santali* and *Ho* languages; Devgam, is trying to forge a script for *Ho* that corresponds to the predominantly oral tradition in *Adivasi* languages.

Critics like Dr. Rajender Thakare, Rose Kerketta, Remis Kandulna, and Doman Sahu "Sameer" have undertaken the evaluation of *Adivasi* literatures. Lataari Kabru Madaavi, who is engaged in the reappraisal of Ravana, is trying to 'set right' the deliberate distortion in the representation of tribal life.

Dr. Gobind Gare in Marathi and Chetanya Prasad Majhi in Orriya, by focusing on the issues of *Adivas*i dislocation, development and change, and Rajender Singh Munda and Ram Dayal Munda by analyzing in Hindi the political and religious contexts of the tribals, are trying to create a blueprint for *Adivasi* studies. Dayamani, Vasavi, Bitiya Murmu, Nirmala Putul and

Rose Kerketta, in trying to pen *Adivasi* questions, are trying to problematize them from different angles.

They are showcasing their folk-literature—bringing to the fore anecdotes, legends, folk tales, writing plays and, simultaneously searching for the tales of heroism. If in '*Haykang* (a *Bori* prayer song), a folk song from Arunachal Pradesh, the priest, while narrating the tale of origin talks about the crime perpetrated on human race by the Creator, then in the 'dirge of the departed souls' the soul of the dead lying in the tomb, instead of craving for heaven, desires to return to the land of the living.

Adivasi writers have also made forays in editing and publication. Their papers and magazines are being published in almost all major languages. In Jharkhand alone about 146 magazines in *Santali* language are being published. The *Aravali Udghosh,* published from Rajasthan—and that has already inspired two special issues of *Yudhrat Aam Aadmi* on *Adivasi* writing—is an important magazine that showcases most of the Hindi speaking *Adivasi* writers.

The *Adivasi* creative ascendance is multifaceted, realistic and has a wide reach or scope. It is a committed writing that aims at social and human well-being premised on democratic and egalitarian bonding and equality. While realizing the importance of education this literature is moving ahead with a mission that seeks to educate and create mass awareness, that can ultimately bring an attitudinal change amongs non-Adivasis and Adivasis.

3

Language Identity in Tribal Areas

A Movement

While on the one hand the issue of language identity in tribal areas has erupted as a movement for sustenance and claiming Adivasi rights a due place from/within the mainstream, on the other hand within the Hindi society and literature, language identity has always remained a controversial issue. The plight of Tulsidas, though in the context of the dominance of Sanskrit, is well known. Rummaging through history in the present context, we are reminded of Ram Vilas Sharma, who on his reflections on language, had put the concept of Hindi *jatiyata* or identity before us, and in the course of time, had expanded on it in the three books that he wrote, to present the notion of Hindi belt.

There are thirty-seven dialects in all within the Hindi belt. Ram Vilas Sharma's notion has posed a great danger to the existence of these dialects and has dealt a blow to 'language claim' of dialects such as *Braj, Avadhi, Maithali, Bhojpuri, Magadhi, Kanauji, Bagri, Kurmali, Nagpuria, Khorta* etc. Because of the pervasiveness of this notion of Hindi (as advanced by Sharma), the claim of these dialects for inclusion in the Eighth Schedule was sidestepped or pushed to the margins. Of late, *Maithali* has been accepted as 'scheduled language' but *Braj, Avadhi, Bhojpuri* and *Rajasthani* and all other languages of Hindi belt have lagged behind, despite an abundance of significant literature that has been written in these languages.

Though there were 146 registered magazines in *Santali* in Jharhkand alone, in 2002, yet this language was not included in the Eighth Schedule. Since then the number of *Santali* publications has increased manifold. They have used these little magazines to develop their contemporary 'written' literature as an activist strategy/struggle for the inclusion of their language in the Eighth Schedule.[1]

Similarly, besides *Assamese*, there are *Bodo, Karbi, Rabha, Garo* languages in Assam that are exclusively spoken by tribals and in which literature is being created. This literature has mainly come to the fore through little magazines. Having no separate scripts of their own, the speakers of these languages began writing borrowing *Assamese* or Roman scripts; now they have even modified and adapted *Devnagari* for the purpose of writing. They have kept their languages not only alive but have also enriched them through the medium of little magazines and newspapers. Apart from *Bodo*, all other tribal languages of Northeastern states are non-scheduled. Bodos had put up an unprecedented fight for *Bodo* language. *Bodo*-speakers not only wrote their stories, poems, myths, folk songs, travelogues, biographies and plays in hundreds but they have also translated the classics from Hindi, Sanskrit and English into *Bodo*. Most of their literature was published in little magazines, dailies and fortnightly newspapers. Through their struggle, *Bodo* people compelled the state government to make provision for their education in their mother tongue. They directed their intellectual movement through little magazines; or in other words, this intellectual movement was possible because of little magazines and newspapers. *Bodo* language too has been included in the Eighth Schedule recently. State administration and Government did not support the growth of *Bodo* literature. Primarily co-coordinated by *Bodo Sahitya Sabha*, its success has been the result of the collective effort of Bodo society, intellectuals, public, workers and little magazines.

If people in Arunachal Pradesh write in Assamese, *Devnagari* and Roman script; people in Meghalaya use Roman script for *Khasi* language. All the languages of Northeastern states, in which literature is being written, are growing either with the help of several little magazines or because of state patronage to their efforts—the Centre is still ignoring them.

As all other languages among eight Northeastern states, except *Bodo*, are non-scheduled, the intellectuals of these states are worried about their getting extinct, despite recognition by the respective states.

M.R. Lahary traces the reason for this crisis of non-scheduled languages, barring a few, in their not being the media of education by which they could have been conserved or nurtured.[2] The government is utterly indifferent to their conservation or their being the media of education. There is also something else to this 'demise' of these languages. It inheres in the adoption, by the native speakers, of other languages at the cost of their own language. Bilingualism prevails in fifty per cent of the tribals. Two contradictory forces are at work within one language/linguistic community—the forces of continuity (holding onto) and that of change. Both of these forces work together. If on the one hand the force of custody conserves the language, the force of change, on the other hand, destroys it. There has been a mushrooming of new contact languages at many places in tribal areas. Actually, whenever a language becomes the medium of education or the medium of literature, it enriches itself by borrowing words from other languages, and never dies.

If non-scheduled languages fulfil any of the following conditions, the possibility of it subjugation by another language is nullified:

1. Language as medium of education, in other words existence of enough avenues for education and development in mother tongue.
2. Language as medium of written literature and medium of compilation of folk literature.
3. Validation of the usefulness of the language and its constant use in practice by its native speakers.

The fulfilment of first condition normally rests with the government, especially with the Central Government. Personal efforts at social level can also be fruitful in achieving it. Speakers of *Bodo* and *Santali*, by creating literature in these languages and by adopting methods of agitation, succeeded in getting these languages as media of education, and also got them enlisted in the Eighth Schedule. In Bengal, it was the state government that took initiative in making *Santali* the medium of education. *Santali* people have even evolved their own script. Following them, scripts have also been developed for *Kudux* and *Ho* languages in Jharkhand, and a large amount of literature is being written in these languages. However, all these efforts are being carried out at social and literary front exclusively. Little magazines are making a significant contribution in this.

R.P. Lama, a Lepcha expert and speaker, quoting from Sir George Grierson's book *Linguistic Survey of India*, opines, "India has 179 major languages and 544 dialects spoken by different groups and subgroups. Out of the 18 Indian languages constitutionally recognized by the Government of India as National languages, no tribal language has found a place."[3] Though *Bodo* and *Santali* have since been listed in the Eighth Schedule, yet this is not enough.

According to Ganesh N. Devy, "9 crore tribals, 6 crore nomads—that is approximately 14-15 crore tribal people are being displaced in the name of development. One or two per cent of the people that form the 'creamy layer' have hijacked everything out of them. The government doesn't have any concrete plan to conserve these languages. Nevertheless, several important magazines of tribal languages are being published in nine or ten languages. A new interrogative articulation is taking shape in the literature of the entire northeast, and southeast, and also in *Munda* and *Gond* literature. It is important for us to understand that tribal literature is emerging as a big challenge to Indian literature. This is not complementary but a complete literature. It straddles at least 90 languages whereas English literature is limited to only one language and European literature to 25 languages. What we have been designating as Indian literature for the past fifty years constitutes only 26 languages, including Pali and Sanskrit."[4]

A literature that encapsulates at least three to four thousand years old history and a wonderful diversity and abundance of communities, and is composed in 90 languages doesn't exist anywhere else in the world—neither in American Black literature, nor Australian nor Negroid. It is a unique chapter in the history of world literature. This is an altogether different phenomenon in world history. Located within such a context, it is a big challenge, not only for the tribals, but also for literature and little magazines, to affect transformation. A challenge that is much bigger in scope than the one that was faced by Black literature. '*Yudhrat Aam Aadmi,*' as peoples' magazine and as a movement has taken up this challenge. By publishing their works in original and in translation, the journal has brought this subaltern literature into national limelight with the view to sustain it and transform it into an empowering tool to pressurize the government into changing the policies.

Since the whole of this literature is being written in non-scheduled—and not in scheduled or recognized—languages, it enjoys no facility for the conservation or custody of these languages. The threat that these languages may either become extinct or may be assimilated is very real. All tribal languages in South have already been absorbed or assimilated in the state or regional languages; they no more exist as written languages. Now they either exist as 'oral' languages or have been confined to certain places and tribes only. *Goreboli* is a language of nomadic tribes such as *Banjara, Lambari* etc., and people of these communities speak this language all over the world. They also tend to imbibe the language of the place they go to as a medium of contact. But, despite being the language of 8 crore people, *Goreboli* is neither accepted as the medium of education nor has it been able to draw the attention of little magazines. However, now they have started writing in their own language and are also bringing out their magazines. The other folk/tribal/local languages of South have, nevertheless, become extinct. At best they only survive as the medium of intra-community dialogue here and there.

Jawaharlal Nehru had said, "Language should not be a dividing factor but it should bring us together and each language can help the other languages of India grow through contact and exchange of ideas."[5] Despite Nehru's lofty thoughts, his government did not pay heed to these languages.

Some of the prominent writers, philosophers, intellectuals and linguists of these non-scheduled languages have expressed their dissatisfaction as to this indifference towards these languages.

Nand Dev Verma, a *Kokborok* speaker and tribal writer from Tripura laments that '*Rajani Kok*' (the language of the kings) language that *Halam* tribes have been speaking, along with many other languages of Tripura, has now been reduced to a minority status within its own state.

In a tone of self-criticism in the context of English domination, Desmond Kharmawphlang, a poet from Meghalya says:

> My burdensome English learning
> Assails me, and the tomb it has become
> Laughs and cackles without end[6]

A poet from Meghalya, who writes poetry in English, says that he can't recite a poem before an audience comprising his own people nor can he enjoy their applause because they do not know English. So he feels guilty.

Nitai Rabha, a poet from *Rabha* community alerts his people to speak their own language:

> Trying to speak *Lema* (Assamese)
> You have lost your tongue—your own dialect
> Our dialect is deficient in no way
> In sweetness
> Then why mimic others?

Praban Bargoyari, a *Boro* writer and an eminent educationist from Assam believes that:

> Except Manipuri, all languages of Indo-monogoloids and Austric groups have been squarely neglected and deprived of their due priority and protection under the provisions of the Constitution of India. I am afraid, such discrimination has encroached upon the fundamental rights of the tribal people of India. In this case, even the

> fundamental rights of Indian Constitution are found self-contradictory. Whereas the Constitution itself guarantees the rights of preservation, adoption and promotion of their language, culture, and religion etc. to its each and every citizen; on the other hand, it squarely discriminated and except Manipuri, included the highly developed Aryan and Dravidian languages only in the 8th Schedule of the Constitution of India.[7]

The threat to non-scheduled languages has, in fact, agitated the entire intellectual class of the Northeast. They believe this danger is the outcome of those government policies that, in conjunction with the processes of globalization, have always tended to profane the local. Religion is yet another factor that at times endangers the existence of these languages in this region. Sometimes regionalism too hinders the development of these tribal languages.

U.G. Brahma (former M.P.) sees privatization of education as a tool of linguistic imperialism in the Indian context. As a result, he opines, "in a dramatic development, there is a mushroom growth of private educational institutes having non-tribal language as the medium of instruction in tribal area and they have threatened seriously the existence of tribal languages as medium of instruction."[8]

As to the question of threat to tribal languages, M.R. Lahary thinks that:

> 'Each of these languages which could not flourish beyond their speaker's areas due to lack of scope for wider use on national level, is endowed with vital potential to add something to national integration just like drops of water, however small, augment the surface of rivers and streams. Linguistic compartmentalization, chauvinism and snobbery weaken the fabric of national integration. It begets not only misgivings but also dislikes among speakers of different languages.'[9]

That is why Brahma expects from the government that it "envisage minimum common national programme for the preservation and development of the non-scheduled languages. Terms and conditions should be relaxed to accommodate some more languages in the 8th Schedule." [10]

It is, thus, not only government policies but also cultural assault from outside that endangers these languages. Tribal communities fear that their original languages or their very linguistic core will be sidelined or destroyed in the name of national educational policy. More than five hundred tribes live in India. Of these, 75 tribal groups that live in different states outside Northeast, barring a few, most of them have either lost their language or are on the verge of losing them; in most cases these have been subsumed within the language of the majority.

Casting doubts on the present education policy, U.G. Brahma says:

> 'In one sense the present education policy is technology based job oriented education, where technical education has been given much prominence. It is often said as need based education also. Sometimes, it is feared that something is hiding behind the new education policy of this government. What is being hidden, I am not aware of that. But if it is again to marginalize the tribal languages by way of forceful interaction or silent means of assimilation, then this is not to be considered a part of the education policy. Because, if any policy is adopted that is not in conformity with the basic principle, it never yields a good result... In the last [60] years of our independence, equal and proportionate development could not be possible and large disparities in development level in various aspects between the weaker and stronger sections have been crystallized more.'[11]

Anil Boro questions, "If a small minority of few thousands enjoy constitutional right to safeguard their language, why not these indigenous languages enjoy the right to safeguard their languages?"[12]

If Jharkhandi magazines could survive today despite the well orchestrated assault of market economy, the credit for it goes to the linguistic pride of its people and their sustained struggle for it. From the time of undivided Bihar to the creation of present day Jharkhand, all successive governments at the Centre and in the state have been shying away from granting due respect to Jharkhandi languages.

By nurturing a consciousness for mother tongues, the language movement, through little magazines and newspapers, can turn into an enabling resistance towards indifference of the government towards tribal and those languages that are on the verge of extinction. Since it is deep rooted, it can stop any linguistic imperialism—native or foreign; be it internal or external colonialism. This consciousness trickles down to the last unit, at least to the literates. Its benefits also reach those illiterate groups of people whose children and relatives have become educated. These little magazines and newspapers and little booklets have contributed a lot in the development and sustenance of indigenous/tribal languages, in their respective areas. The articles and issues that appear in their own language in these magazines, keep alive their faith even when these people move out of their states. These language magazines thus keep inspiring them to keep their speech and script alive even in the *pardes* or the alien land. These people continue to publish their language magazine from big cities like Mumbai, Chennai, Kolkata, Guwahati etc. A large number of such little magazines of distant and far-flung languages are also printed in Delhi and other big cities; these keep intact their touch with their own language even after moving to Delhi or Bombay or any other big city. They earn their livelihood through Hindi or English; they even converse in these languages but think, plan, protest and resolve in their own language. And it is this that keeps their languages alive. Consequently, our priority should be the encouragement of their 'language' literature, whether in original or in translation, through the medium of little magazines and string them—the non-scheduled, unlisted or listed, indigenous languages—together symbiotically and relationally, **so that they can enrich major languages and get enriched in turn through them. Linguistic democracy is only**

possible if the major language works with the intention of enriching, and in turn getting enriched by other language, and not with the intention of swamping or killing it.

Once upon a time, realizing Bangla's hegemony, Assamese speakers rose in protest against it. It was only because of this struggle for language pride in the wake of the awakening of language consciousness, that underdeveloped/ backward languages could remain alive. Assamese also got its due place. *Kokborok* in Tripura and *Mizo* in Mizoram could become state-languages because of the affirmative polices of the respective governments. In Arunachal Pradesh, Hindi or Assamese are used as official languages. There is no place for indigenous languages despite they being a dozen in number. The *Apatani* and *Aadi-Sherdukpen* speaking tribes have started writing in Hindi, Assamese or English out of shear compulsion, for their languages neither enjoy any patronage, nor do they have any script. But why is it so?

One can enumerate many reasons for this state of affairs. One of the major reason among these is the non-existence of scripts in these languages. People in northeast have, nevertheless, begun scripting the literature in their own language by adopting the Roman or Devnagari script or of some of other major regional languages. As a result their languages and dialects are still safe. By using diacritical marks in consonance with their own sounds and symbols on the available scripts, they have improvised a language that is grammatically and phonetically viable—and have started writing their literature in it. This is how they have inked their literature. All these, however, are individual initiatives. There has been no help, whatsoever, from the government. This love for their language has not only made them conscious about it, but has also taught them to oppose linguistic authoritarianism. They have turned rebels. The protest against Hindi in South, Bengali in Assam, and revolt against Assamese by tribal people are signs of emerging language consciousness/identity.

Tribal communities are not opportunistic like the mainstream communities. It is free from casteism or middle class mentality. Though weak economically and politically, it is nevertheless equipped with the feeling of equality and co-operation. It is this awareness of one's identity and self-respect that has forced the Dalits to struggle. Dalits didn't have any identity on the language plane; for them the issue of freedom, which could get them identity and self-respect, was more important than the issue of language identity. Nevertheless, on literary front they are engaged in struggle on 'art-for-art' and 'art-for-life' sake issues, or in other words, on the issues of form and content *versus* reality and authenticity.

The middle class of Hindi belt possesses the resources of Hindi and English to earn its livelihood and to improve its life-style, but the tribals—located on the lowest rung of the ladder—have no option other than limited reservation. It is therefore imperative to create opportunities for them in their own language.

Imperial thinking is authoritarian; it not only usurps the languages but also creates animosity among them. Translation is a necessary condition for the growth of languages and to crash language imperialism. Translation has the potential to link and acquaint languages with each other in ways that they can stand together against the domination of anyone language.

Even in other countries the middle class remains an opportunistic class. Poor or rich, high caste or low, majority people of Hindi belt are the custodians and propagators of middle class mentality. And it is this middle class that ironically revolts as well as leads too. In the process of fine-tuning Hindi into an administrative/state language, the intellectuals and writers of Hindi have made it lean heavily on Sanskrit. Consequently, it is no more a language of the common people. On the other hand, genuine Hindi, a combination of *Khariboli* and Urdu, and tampered with by the local dialects, which was known as Hindustani—has become *Janbhasa*, or the language of the masses. It is this Hindustani that is in fact used as link language throughout the country. The so called stalwarts of Hindi belt, in their manoeuvres to prove Urdu as the language of the Muslims, have wittingly or unwittingly, turned Hindi into the language of Hindus. To our great surprise this very Hindi became our national or administrative language. It also became the self-proclaimed language of great literature, and common man's language, *i.e.*, Hindustani, was reduced into the language of folk or inferior literature. The priority should have been the development of people's language. It was this language that originating in *dakhini* dialect had joined hand with Urdu to evolve into *khariboli*. The original *khariboli* had words from all the dialects which are either used/spoken in various pronunciations in different languages including Panjabi or are still intact/present in their original form even today. The words of *khariboli* are present in Marathi and Gujarati too. But after donning the robe of Sanskrit it has attained the status of *bhasa* or language and has attained status as national language, but, in the process, has got severed from the *jan* or the people.

The new generation of the present is busy acquiring employment friendly language or languages and it is in these languages that literature is being written. Having been accepted by government job and global market it has also become the language of media, and is once again changing its contours.

If we want to save/conserve these languages/dialects then it calls for ushering in of language democracy and creation of opportunities for non-scheduled languages. Though it can be achieved easily and swiftly with the help of the concerned state, if and only if the state can provide for need based education in the medium of these languages and it also encourages literature created in these languages, yet even without government support a desire to protect their language identity and culture has kindled the consciousness of tribals and has led them to produce realistic and issue oriented literature incorporating new cultural values. The spread of education and availability of scripts in a few languages, coupled with an awareness of impending danger to their identity, has whetted their consciousness with a hunger for writing and publication in these languages. They have effectively employed little magazines and newspapers as media to raise these issues.

If every magazine dedicates a few pages to anyone of these non-scheduled languages for translation, language sisterhood could be created. The authoritarian, imperialistic language bias creates animosity among languages because by imposing itself on other it tends to usurp the other; the language sisterhood, on the other hand, promotes the tendency to reciprocate, or mutual give and take among languages. It believes in democracy where every one has the right to live and let live and grow together. Through translation, little magazines can create an atmosphere of linguistic sisterhood and unity among them.

NOTES

1. Since the writing of this work, Santali has been included in the Eighth Schedule of the Constitution.
2. For details see M.R. Lahary, "Future of Unscheduled Tribal Languages," *Sannidhi*, 34-44.
3. George Grierson quoted in R.P. Lama,"The Role of Tribal Linguistic Groups in Implementation of Education Policy," *Sannidhi*, 51.
4. G.N. Devy, "Adivasi Samaj Aur Sahitya Ki Chunautiyan" *Yudharat Aam Aadmi: Akhil Bhartiya Adivasi Sahitya Sammelan*—Special Issue No. 80: 23-24.
5. Jawaharlal Nehru quoted in Lama, 49.
6. New Frontiers 2.1 (Winter 2000) 103.
7. Praban Bargoyari, "Future of Tribal Languages in 21st Century and Their Role in Strengthening National Integration," *Sannidhi*, 46.
8. U.G. Brahma, "Tribal and Their Education: An Overview," *Sannidhi*, 10.
9. For details see M.R. Lahary, "Future of Unscheduled Tribal Languages," *Sannidhi*, 38-39.
10. U.G. Brahma, "Tribal and Their Education: An Overview," *Sannidhi*, 10
11. U.G. Brahma, "Tribal and Their Education: An Overview," *Sannidhi*, 8.
12. Anil Boro, "Indigenous Languages of North East India: Threats to Their Survival," *Sannidhi*, 32.

4

The Problematic of Tribal Identity

It was the Communist Party (Marxist) of India that, for the first time, took a lead to comprehensively deliberate on the problems that common people in the Hindi belt face, and to find their solutions. In its 18th extended session spread over seven days, the party had extensive discussions on different problems and concerns of the masses. Many prominent scholars from all over India shed light on the issues of mass culture, education, religion, democracy, nation and globalization from different angles. This seven day long conference was not a mere formality; its concerns were substantial. It did not confine itself to mere lamentation or cataloguing of complaints. All the scholars, in their unique way, suggested remedies to prevent and redress the problems. The highlight of the conference was the solemnity with which it focused on the issues and problems of Dalits, women, minorities and tribal people. So far no party had cared to give so much prominence to the people placed on the margins. Even in 21st century the attitude of so-called civilized world to these oppressed groups is primitive. It is imperative to examine the notion of their identity closely.

If on the one hand, the question of tribal identity is intimately related to the 'definition' of their name, on the other, it is deeply enmeshed with their social structure and the sources of their livelihood, *i.e.*, water, forest, land etc. If their origin validates or affirms their identity, it is their heritage, language, education, culture and life-style that keep it alive. Their identity cannot be protected without preserving all these. And as Nehru had put it aptly, the preservation of their identity demands, 'non-imposition of our culture on them.' Till date we have thought only in terms of teaching them; we have never tried to learn from their democratic and egalitarian system. Instead of imposing our half-baked or immature culture and civilization on them, we need to learn from them the real meaning of value based society, freedom, equality and brotherhood.

One of the major differences that distinguishes Dalit situation from that of the tribal inheres in the manner in which both were ousted from mainstream culture and civilization. Infact Dalits were ousted from the village boundary and were forced to live a life of humiliating subordination, sans self-respect or human dignity and were branded as 'other', within Indian culture, whereas tribals were boycotted from the very civilization and were pushed into the jungles. While Dalits were excommunicated from mainstream culture, the tribal people were ex-communicated from civilization. Yet tribals did have their forest and land with them, and kept intact the legacy of their culture and continued to live with dignity and self-respect. But now even that their cultural and social structure and their autonomy and independence are endangered. Their self-reliance and self-respect is shaken and they are becoming victims of inferiority complex.

It is often said that when 'a tribal speeks–he sings–when a tribal walks–he dances', but this is not the whole truth. When he is angry, it is not his tongue but his hand carrying bow and arrows, that moves. When he confronts an opponent, he is capable of vanquishing him just like Chitrangda's son Barbarik, who having vanquished Arjuna in the wrestling duel secured him with a rope. Nevertheless, it is a fact that Aryan imperialism has always deceived, cheated, looted and suppressed the tribal and pushed him to the forest. This has happened throughout the world. The main factor behind it has been the expansionism, authoritarianism and domination of the empires. These factors combined to drive him far away from civilization into the forests, turned him into an exhibit, and compelled him to keep mum for centuries. If he was allowed to speak, it was only in the language of Hanuman (a disciple of Rama) who spoke the language of Ram–an Indian king who is considered God's incarnation and not in the language of his *Bonga*–spirit of tribal ancestor. In other words, he was supposed to mimic the dominant or was forced to articulate in the selfish language of the stranger or outsider. Now, however, he has seen through this hegemonic stratagem and has thus started speaking in his own language, or in other words, has taken steps towards self-validating articulation.

One cannot imagine tribal existence without forests and land. That's why the ruling clique from the plains, or rulers and administrators from India or abroad had conspired cunningly to separate him from land and forest. In the subsequent paragraphs I intend to explain it in detail.

Who is a tribal? It is a question that impinges on their identity and history. To answer it, we shall have to begin by problematizing the term mentioned in Constitution of India—*janjati* (literally a tribe or a community with an indigenous caste), for this term not only misleads us but also cast a doubt and put a question mark on their very identity or self-respect. When tribals have no *jati* or caste, how can they be termed as people with a particular caste or a *jati*. They may be called a tribe or a community but by no stretch of imagination–a *jati*. For quite some time now, by baptizing them as *Banwasi* or the forest dwellers, and by raising a slogan of 'come back home,'—it literally means 'Come back to Hinduism.' The religious and communal groups in our country have been conspiring to erase the identity of the tribals. Alternatively these forces have also been planning to homogenize their culture and assimilate it in the mainstream, by setting one tribal against another in the name of religion. Steins episode in Orissa, transformation of *Johar* into *Jai Shree Ram* in Gujarat are living examples of this tendency. The truth is that Adivasis were never Hindus nor they had any religion or God. They always had a way of life nor they have a temple or worshipping place for any deity. If at all they regard or worship anything it is nature, trees or the spirit of their ancesstors living in rocks.

The previous government led by Prime Minister Vajpai went so far as to deny the very existence of tribals in India before UNO. The term *Banwasi* not only challenges the origin and source of tribals, but also echoes a suggestion of their being uncivilized, beastly and backward. Thus it diffuses their claim of being indigenous. Generally speaking, a non-tribal too can be a '*Banwasi*', *e.g.* Ram has been called a '*Banwasi*'. As such, this term and its usage tends to make *Adivasis* suspicious as regards to its motive—isn't it a conspiracy to pin down or diffuse their identity?

UNO in its Declaration on the Rights of the Indigenous People defines indigenous people as the "descendants of people who have inhabited the present territory of a country wholly or partially at the time when the persons of a different culture or ethnic origin arrived from other parts of the world, overcame them by conquest, settlement or other means and reduced them to non-dominant or colonial conditions."[1] People in India too believe that tribals are 'aboriginals' of Indian origin or the indigenous inhabitants of India. They do not follow Aryan or Hindu culture. People from plains (in India) have been envisioning them as beasts; they have been depicted as animal-like creatures with long teeth, horns and tails in Indian scriptures. They have also been insulted as demons and monsters. People in West called them Pagan, and by identifying them as tribes made them feel beastly and thus humiliated them. Thus, instead of treating them as human, both the civilizations—Oriental or Occidental—were bent on treating them as beastly creatures. In the course of time, two factors—protests by tribal people and the change in human consciousness with the emergence of humanism in the wake of industrialization—forced some rulers, though in their own vested interests, to reframe rules ostensibly for tribal welfare. British rulers in India aptly exemplified this mindset. Nevertheless, despite being a vanquished entity, *Adivasis* have kept alive their cultural heritage, their language, and their collective traditions and life-mores. Nature is their friend or co-inhabitant. Their *Bonga,* who is their ancestor, exists in trees and rocks. No temple is dedicated to it. The *Bonga* is invited to eat and drink with their family. *Sakhua* trees form their *Sarna* (The sacred place). They worship *Jaherthan* or *Sasaan,* or big rocks erected adjacent to each other or that naturally exist nearby, in memory of their ancestors. Their religion forms their life style—it is neither a faith nor a blind worship with them. Their unique legacy and identity is founded on democracy and autonomy that revolves around collective life-mores, equality, liberty and fraternity. They have their own languages. They have their own different cultures with their origin mainly in Austric and Dravidian sources. *Bodos*, who originated from the land of Mongols, had arrived earlier in Assam than Aryans. Recently it is being said that *Mizos* originally belong to Israel. *Mundas* who, later split into four subgroups—*Munda, Santal, Ho and Kharia*—trace their ancestry to Mohen-jodaro. *Oraons* are Dravidians. Lot of words from *Mundari* and *Santali* languages are found even in *Vedas*. It is an evidence of their languages being older than Sanskrit. In fact many languages seem to have originated from these languages and not from Sanskrit, as is often claimed. Still, Sanskrit is considered to be the mother of all languages in India. The researchers focus only on Sanskrit. The research in source languages is non-existent; consequently their very existence is endangered today.

To reiterate, the tribal identity is intricately enmeshed with their right to the forest, land, water and natural resources. Their languages, culture, community life-style, tradition and rituals, and their four-levelled democratic judicial system are very important to their existence. To provide them with their existential props mentioned above; it is necessary that they be given back their rights to self-determination, autonomous government and self-rule in accordance with the U.N. manifesto.

Jawaharlal Nehru had said once, "The problem of problems is not to disturb the harmony of tribal life and simultaneously to work for its advance; not to impose anything on the tribals and simultaneously to work for their integration as members and part of the Indian society."[2] We need not go very far to grasp Nehru's motive in this statement. According to Nehru, "We are welcome to our way of living, but why impose it on others... I am not sure at all which is the better way of living... the tribal or our own. In some respects I am quite certain that theirs is better. Therefore, it is grossly impertinent on our part to approach them with an air of superiority, to tell them how to behave or what to do. There is no point of trying to make them second rate copy of ourselves"[3]. But the irony of the fact is that after independence, the ruling clique has demolished the social structure of tribals and has created obstacles in their harmonious life; a number of anti-tribal enactments were imposed on them. So the question of India's unhindered and complete integration has remained unresolved till date. By ignoring them, we can neither understand the multiple problems of tribals nor can we solve them. Hence we'll have to weigh our policies against the weight of these questions. We'll have to examine whether or not India as a republic, society, and state has made and implemented tribal welfare policies in sync with their aspirations by confronting their questions head on.

It is true that during the times of *Mahabharata* or even prior to that, having ousted them from civilization, Aryans had pushed tribals into jungles but after the advent of the British, the nature of this intervention changed. Things got even worse after independence. Earlier the people in power would dominate tribals but would not interfere with their internal organization and life-style or rituals.

Before independence, moneylenders, feudals and trading classes from Indian plains sucked the tribals dry and evicted them from their lands. The tribal community was wedged between double colonialism, both internal and external. In fact the internal dominance was far crueler than the external. The onslaught of this double colonialism reduced the tribals into a minority on their own home turf. It also created a class of displaced tribals.

A tribal sans land and forest is a tribal without identity. In depriving them of land and forest, the English erased their identity, and after independence our governments too continued with the same policy. The system of permanent settlement formed the bedrock of British revenue policy. The English used it to hand over land rights to *zamindars*. In the process, the tribals, who were the joint masters of the whole village, became bonded ryots of *zamindars* for successive generations. In course of time, *zamindars*, moneylenders and non-tribals had the tribal-land transferred in their names by hook or by crook. This manipulation of theirs rendered tribals into landless bonded labour.

They were once the 'kings' of the forest. Now they have been converted into wood-thieves. The wood-buying outsiders have become the 'kings' of the forests. The tribal had *khutkatti* rights over forest and land; that means they had the rights to clear the forest to prepare cultivable patch of land for their own use. Now with dwindling forests and modification in CNT Act (that had the provision to ban the transfer of tribal land), their right to land stands abolished.

For the supply of their needs like *latha* (a wooden pole like contraption used for taking out water from the deep well) *chhavan* (thatch material) and firewood, a part of the forest abundant for their needs, was reserved for them. But the British commercialized the forests and after independence, Indian governments too followed the same policy. Consequently, a number of contractors were contracted to fell the forests and the forest vanished. As a result, the tribals were not only deprived of sources of their livelihood, but were also deprived of *latha* to water their fields, *chhavan* for their shelters (homes) and firewood for their hearths/cooking. These things became rare or went beyond their reach. Their sustenance was dependant on the produce of the forests. They could survive the drought or flood or the good and bad times on flowers of *sakhua* trees. But now in place of *sakhua*, eucalyptus and teak trees are being planted for commercial purposes. In 1980s, the tribals of Santal Pargana had actively revolted against this policy.

The forest dependent sources of tribal livelihood included extraction of oil from *mahua* flowers and its seeds, *kusum* and *plas* flowers for making dyes and colours. Collecting of gum was done from the bark of *plas* trees. Herb based medical practice, making *pattals* (Plates of leaves for eating) and *bidis* from leaves, and cutting *datoons* or twig-brushes from branches of various bushes were their sources of living. These sources of livelihood have been virtually destroyed by 'developmental activities' such as reckless felling of jungles, building of dams and adoption of open cast mines etc. specially in coal sector in these areas. The difficulties of the tribals were further compounded by the government enactments of 1979 that apart from fixing boundaries also imposed a ban on their entry into the forest. These enactments compelled them to flee away from their places, and as a result today we have approximately sixty thousand tribal girls who are working as domestic servants in Delhi. Only twenty thousand of these girls have been traced so far by an agency from Jharkhand.

In 1960-61 Dheber Commission had commented, "A tribal who considered himself to be master of the forest, was reduced into a ryot as part of a well planned scheme. He has been left to the mercy of forest department... and what were thought to be rights or special rights in 1894 were reinterpreted as concessions in 1952. The narrow aim that considers commercial gains as the biggest gain has been the chief cause of the destruction and exploitation of forests. Indisputably this system/structure/policy/thinking has impacted the tribals negatively. Tribals' rights to land and forest were violently usurped in the name of national interest. In fact the national interest was nothing but selfishness of powerful class."[4] The sources of employment dwindled. Tribals were rendered into a class of cheap labour and, taking advantage of this, people from outside burdened them with slavery. This is how—for the growth of capitalists and for the commercial exploitation of the forests—a large number of tribals were reduced into helpless and hapless beings. A conspiracy was deliberately hatched to turn tribals into cheap labour to be used as a cog in the exploitative machine for the benefit of the capitalistic class.

A tribal may not be aware of the benefits of this development, but he knows for sure that this development has destroyed him. Due to the resultant tribal displacement, he had to leave his home and land. This displacement nearly finished his language and culture. But even those who stayed back in their land, they too, because of the influx of people from outside, became a minority in their own region. This happened in states like Chhatisgarh and Jharkhand. This also affected their culture and language. Many of them adopted the language of the majority and got assimilated into it.

Today, in the name of development, the Government of India has acquired their land extensively and has uprooted them. Consequently, they have started moving out to other states in search of employment at a great risk of losing their language and culture. Alternatively, having been displaced within their own home turf, they are compelled to become landless and bonded labour.

Interestingly, tribals' dwellings have been areas of abundant natural resources. Uranium or coal, mica or iron, copper or manganese, all these minerals are found in abundance in tribal dominated states, especially in Hindi region. Being hilly terrains or plateaus, not only streams but '*nads*' (masculine gender for river) too flow through these. If Northeast has Brahmaputra, Jharkhand has Damodar flowing through it. The government has built big dams on these rivers in the name of development. As a result millions of people were displaced, especially in Jharkhand and Bengal. The county's development policies should have been egalitarian, or in other words, they should have aimed at equitable development. But people did not get equal share in development. The development took place but for select few at the cost of majority, especially at the cost of tribals. The tribals, through acquisition of their land, were not only uprooted in the name of national development, but their constitutionally sanctioned fundamental rights were also infringed upon. These development projects also disturbed the economic balance of these tribal states/regions. Not only this, the government brought in many Bills in 1998. Land Acquisition Amendment Bill was brought in hurriedly to pave way for the covert handing over of the land of their choice to MNCs. It accelerated the pace and process of displacement in the country, thereby making available cheap labour in a large number to the capitalists.

> There was a prohibition on the acquisition of tribal land under acts such as Land Acquisition and Chhotanagpur

> Tenancy Act. The government amended these acts arbitrarily just to get rid of certain provisions in them. Because of this government-policy between 1991 and 1995, 150 million people had been dislocated from 50 thousand acres of land in Jharkhand alone; out of these 41.27 per cent were tribals. The percentage of tribals displaced under defense schemes is 89.7 per cent; it amounts to 75.2 per cent in water resource projects.

During British times, private owners had taken control over thousands of acres of tribal land for coalmines; this had reduced the erstwhile landowning tribals into cheap labour. To forcibly lay claim to whatever little land tribals were still left with, the government enacted the Coal Bearing Area Act of 1957. After the nationalization of mines, like 'Nilahe' or indigo farming Britishers, the coal companies took possession of the lands of tribals without prior notice and started mining at their own will. They had to forego this forced possession as a result of Supreme Court's stay order as a result of a petition filed by villagers and myself. Our strong movement to this effect also prevented them to take possession of tribal lands in that area. But prior to the stay order hundreds of fields had been turned into mines. The houses were bulldozed. *Mahua* and *saal* trees were uprooted or felled and the 'king' of forest first became 'Ryot' and subsequently turned into a displaced farm hand. Today, having been displaced from his own land, a tribal, in order to survive, is compelled into selling the coal stolen at risk from his own land or from the land that he owned once. Today, he, after loading two tons of coal on his bicycle, hauls it up the valley from Ramgarh to Ranchi and earns meagrely 40 rupees after bribing rupees 10 each to three *thanas* and paying his return fare and the rent for the bicycle, is dubbed as a coal thief. His whole family helps him in stealing this coal—this translates into eight people earning forty rupees a day. With a rope tied to his waist, he is compelled to descend into illegal coalmines, and sometimes when these mines collapse, he is trapped inside and dies. The villagers are afraid of claiming this dead body; lest they should be implicated for coal stealing.

A four-lane expressway is being planned from Ranchi to Behragoda in Jharkhand. It would render 3 lac tribals landless. Where would these people go? Since the government does not have any answer, some of them are taking to arms. Displacement coupled with the submersion of land by dams or its takeover by coalmines, the fear of retrenchment in the wake of closure of other factories—and all such factors are swelling the ranks of unemployed among tribals.

Displacement has always been the main problem tribals have faced in the country. They were chased away earlier too (due to racial and cultural reasons). Today they are being chased away in the name of so called development that actually deprives them of their lands and means of living. Only the methods have changed. Earlier they would have gone from one forest to another but today the forests have either been cleared or tribals' entry in these has been banned; they have also been deprived of all the rights to the produce of forest. Now they are running towards cities.

The question of language is also connected with their identity. The tribals are imparted education in the language of the state and not in their own native languages. The *Bhils* of Rajasthan pronounce *'sa'* as *'ch'*. The tribal from Hazaribagh pronounce *'a'* as *'ya'*. When a *Bhil* child goes to a school, and says *'chamocha'* instead of *'samosa,'* and speaks *'aad'* instead of standard *'yad'* in Hazaribag and Ranchi, he becomes the butt of laughter for the Hindi speaking children, and in desperation he drops out of school. The only way to educate tribals and to protect their language is to teach them in their mother tongue (in schools). Yet another factor that hinders their education is the prevalence of school curriculum that is hostile, unconventional and unconnected to/with their identity. A course book of primary school, in Rajasthan says, "*Bhil* is a thief." The schools located in Hindi regions or other parts of the country teach that the tribals are demons and monsters. While Ramayan is a tale of their humiliation, *Mahabharta* is a narrative that was ostensibly written to deceive them. The mainstream course curriculum thus insults them. Consequently, such education acts as a double-edged sword, while on the one hand it imbues them with an inferiority complex;

on the other it makes them look towards others with suspicion. All this calls for a change in the curricula.

The question of tribal identity is thus intimately related to their problems, and solution to these problems should be our priority or primary agenda. This agenda can be strung together into the following 19-point formulation:

1. Recognition of indigenous/adivasi/tribal peoples' rights to natural resources.
2. Seeking an alternative to the present government policy of 'destruction in the name of development,' protection of land and forest rights, return of the usurped land of the indigenous/adivasi/tribal people and their right to entry into, and to the produce of jungle, along with the right to water, forest and land, and right to *laatha, chhavan* and *jalaavan.*
3. Repeal of law related to the fixing of forest boundary, and deployment of tribals for the protection of jungles.
4. Ban on outsiders' entry and acquisition of land by them in these areas so as to stop them from turning the indigenous/adivasi/tribal people into a minority within their own home turf.
5. A system of self-rule and autonomous government along with financial, educational and administrative rights for indigenous/adivasi/tribal people.
6. Share in and self-determination of developmental schemes to indigenous/adivasi/tribal people.
7. Building up of indigenous/adivasi/tribal people's identity, self-confidence and self-respect; negation of the term *banwasi* and replacement of the word *janjati* with indigenous tribal/adivasi in the Constitution.
8. Investigation, re-writing and research of/in indigenous/adivasi/tribal peoples' history.
9. Removal and re-evaluation of the humiliating portrayal of indigenous/adivasi/tribal people in literature and myths, especially in Indian literature and religious scriptures.

10. To provide for the education of indigenous/adivasi/tribal people in their mother tongue and the encouragement of tribal language, culture, history and literature and their incorporation/inclusion in course-books and curricula.
11. Provision of equal shares of women in property, and equal participation in indigenous/adivasi/tribal culture.
12. Recognition and sanction of indigenous/adivasi/tribal people's contribution in the making of Indian culture and history.
13. Protection to/of indigenous citizens belonging to nomadic and denotified tribes and their constitutional rights, removal of regional restrictions imposed on them/their movement so as to enable them to avail of and enjoy the facilities that belong to them by virtue of their being indigenous/adivasi/tribals anywhere in the country. This rule should also be applicable to those indigenous/adivasi/tribal people who move out to Delhi, Assam or any other place in search of employment, so as to ensure their basic rights.
14. Ban on settling of non-tribal in indigenous/adivasi/tribal areas through infiltration or otherwise so as to prevent internal colonialism.
15. Introduction of special plans, research and studies for the growth and development of neglected primitive tribes
16. Translation of indigenous/adivasi/tribal literature with an aim to create dialogue, discussion and tribal integration.
17. Launching movements against ill effects of globalization on indigenous/adivasi/tribal people.
18. Registration of indigenous/adivasi/tribal people as a separate entity/category in the column of region instead of forcing them to right the prevalent Indian religions, *i.e.* Hindu, Muslim, Christian etc., in government census and other records.
19. Empowerment of women for their participation in the process of decision making on the subject and process

of development for indigenous/adivasi/tribal people; and assurance of gender equality in allied fields. Exclusive schemes and plans for the development of indigenous/adivasi/tribal people.

Note: Autonomous government, self-rule, or self-determination does not mean separation from the country.

NOTES

1. Quoted in B. Pakem, "Indigenous Peoples of North-east India and the United Nations Declaration of the Right of Self-Determination, *Souvenir-K.S.U.* 20th *Anniversary Celebration 1978-1998*: 91.
2. Jawaharlal Nehru quoted in Parban Bargoyary "Future of Tribal Languages in 21st Century and their Role in Strengthening National Integration," *Sannidhi*, the Souvenir on National Conference on Tribal Languages (New Delhi: Gandhi Hindustani Sahitya Sabha, 2003) 45.
3. *Ibid*.

5

Woman in Adivasi Culture and Literature

The myths and illusions regarding the autonomy and independence of *Adivasi* women are rampant. But there is yet another, perhaps lesser known facet to indigenous women; some harsh norms and divisions exist within those *Adivasi* societies that ostensibly make these women feel lesser beings than their male counterparts. Nevertheless, one has to accept that, in contrast to mainstream Indian culture, *Adivasi* women have the freedom to choose their own grooms. They are neither punished nor pronounced guilty for this. Tribal people have had a custom of *Ghotul*, wherein the boys and girls lived together and received all sorts of knowledge. It was their training centre. That's why, in contrast to women elsewhere, Adivasi girls are neither shy nor feel vulnerable in the company of boys; on the contrary they interact with them, weigh or evaluate them, and if they see in them any scope for spending life together, they even marry them. They also have the right to walk out of marriage.

It is, however, with respect to right to property that *Adivasi* women are subjected to harsh rules. To put in proper perspective the question of tribal women, it is pertinent here to understand the past and present context of tribal social organization. Though matriarchy still exists in some tribes but it is patriarchy that generally prevails in most of the tribes. Even in those tribes that follow matriarchy—though the family lineage is matrilineal and at places the daughter inherits the family property, yet it is either the father or the maternal uncle who commands social importance. Their opinions prevail.

By and large *Adivasi* societies believe in equality and community living. Before the advent of the British they did not have any notion of property. The village land that was mainly situated in the forests belonged to the village as a whole, and not to any individual. Everyone, woman, child and old, healthy, handicapped or indisposed, all had equal share in the property, land or the crops. Even in patriarchal tribes, a girl could reside with her parents as long as she desired. The care and maintenance of woman divorced from her husband was the responsibility of the parental family. As no one had an exclusive or separate claim to land, the question of woman's claim to it did not arise. The *Adivasi* community generally lived separately in forests, away from the people living in plains or the so-called civilized society. Their females, who in any case have the capacity to work harder than their men folk—were as independent as the males. Barring a few tribes in Jharkhand and Chhatisgarh who did not allow their women to touch plough or bow or thatching of the roof they did not suffer social discrimination in any other arena of work—whether it involved wood cutting, labouring in the fields or hunting. The problem began when, in the course of time, the English began to register/allot land in the name of *zamindars* under the new revenue policy. Since the land was now registered in the name of men, the tribal head or *Majhi-hadam*, fearing that the land in the name of a woman, after her marriage, would go over to a different home, sabotaged its allotment in her name. At time the land was registered in the name of only one male member of the family, it denied other male members of the family their claim or ownership in it. With the advent of non-tribal people in the tribal areas as land lessee and moneylenders, land and forests passed into their hands. With it the non-tribal malaise and evils seeped into the tribal community replacing their community consciousness with individualistic and monopolistic tendencies. Even today the women of *Santal, Munda, Uraon, Ho* and *Kharia* tribes have no right to parental property. To top it, the women of these tribes are discriminated against even in the distribution of work. According to Bitiya Murmu of Jharkhand—"One could understand and perhaps appreciate if the distribution of work had been based on the physical differences between man and woman but instead of distributing work in accordance with physical capabilities, the 'tribal-patriarchy' does it with an aim to stake claim on woman." To this effect it devises rigorous norms that prohibit woman from jobs such as ploughing the field, touching the bow and thatching of the roof. This barriar is imposed in order to retain their ownership over land and home, which by definition are modern symbols of property. If a woman engages in any such activity, then like Sajoni Kisku, the protagonist of Nirmala Putul's poem, she has either to yoke herself to the plough to till the land or has to eat fodder from the oxen-pan.

In the past few years especially in Jharkhand, the demands for right to paternal property are becoming audible. Juliana Lakra, an Adivasi woman, had approached the Supreme Court with the help of Madhu Kishwar, the editor of *Manushi*, on the issue of this discrimination. On April 17, 1996, the Supreme Court had given an opportunity to the government of Bihar to amend this unjust system, but the government opposed the tribal women's claim to parental property with the plea that *Adivasi* community itself resisted it because it was apprehensive that this amendment would covertly help the non-tribal in grabbing tribal land in the guise of marrying a tribal woman. The Supreme Court directed the governments of Jharkhand also to probe into the issue, but the Tribal Advisory Council of Bihar, on 31.7.1992 had already opposed it. The court once again recommended extensive debate on the issue, but neither the government of Bihar nor that of Jharkhand complied with the order; instead, through their representatives, these governments kept on misleading the Supreme Court.

However, this unjust practice is confined to only a small number of tribal communities. The situation in Northeast is different. In Mizoram women can plough the land. Meghalaya is a matriarchal society. In *Khasi* Tribe, it is the daughter who inherits the property. Even in *Bodo* tribe they are not denied this right. Though patriarchy prevails in *Mizo* community, yet the genealogy is matrilineal. Except in a few tribal groups, such as *Banjaras, Lambadies* or *Kuruppan* gypsies, the tribal communities in the south have, by and large, been absorbed within the regional-cultures. However, some of the things that are common to all *Adivasis* in India include—absence of dowry system, liberty to choose one's groom, freedom to love, and un-inhibited participation in feasting and festivities. Most of the mainstream Indian traditions don't grant these opportunities to their women.

In these *Adivasi* societies man can only marry by paying the bride price. In Jharkhand the custom is known as *Paunpratha*. In Santal tribes groom's side has to pay the bride-price and has also to gift an ox/bull to bride's brother. Groom's family is also expected to treat the bride-side according to the latter's demands and wishes. All these factors might have given rise to the custom of marrying a girl after eloping with her among *Santal* people. As a consequence many *Santali* women remain unmarried for long. This custom has also resulted in inter-tribe marriage among them. Bitiya Murmu says: "It is simply unjust to deny property-rights to *Adivasi* woman on the basis of customary laws. The change in laws may lead to bitterness or opposition; but the fact is that the reactionary social segments tend to terrorize, whenever the basic structures are sought to be changed or whenever the downtrodden are given their rights. Hence, for affirmative reforms, the social welfare state will have to confront them firmly."

Adivasi women are self-reliant. They work hard for the sustenance of their families. Since tribal women have no property rights in these tribes, it is a common practice to brand such women who are either deserted by their husbands, are widows or are out spoken, as Dayans, *i.e.*witches. Thus they are tortured, humiliated and degraded socially in front of everybody and ultimately killed. Witch tradition is thus an offshoot of a slant towards patriarchal dominance and the absence of female right to property. If a girl becomes a widow, she along with her child/children, is killed to escape the burden of her maintenance, a right that is rightfully hers.

Recently, under Maheshwar *thana* in Jharakhand, Narayan Kisku's sixty-five years old widow was murdered by her brother-in-law with an intention of grabbing her land.

It is in fact the tribal man, who has been transferring his land to the non-tribal people in lieu of liquor or to pay off debt. Hence the tribal logic that the land would get transferred to non-tribals once they marry the tribal girls is untenable. A minor amendment in the law—"that in the case of a tribal woman marrying a non-tribal, the tribal wife and her own children would only inherit the tribal land of their mother and not the husband who is a non-tribal"—would easily take care of this 'logic'.

In Rajasthan there exits a tribal-*panchayat* for 28 villages—it is called *Atthaeesa, i.e.* a group of twenty-eight. Within its jurisdiction if a *Meena* man murders another *Meena* man, his family is exiled as punishment. However, if a *Meena* woman is killed by a *Meena* man, the same *panchayat*, instead of pronouncing a punishment commensurate with the nature of crime, takes a very lenient view and only recommends a dip of penitence in the holy Ganges, an offering of one and quarter kilograms of roasted gram and jaggery, and one and quarter kilogram of *jowar* for the pigeons. *Meena* panchayat would rather punish one who is guilty of fratricide instead of the one who is guilty of murdering a woman. This only reflects an unjust and misogynist patriarchal mindset.

Though Khasi is a matriarchical society but according to J. Shangpiliang, a *Khasi* writer—"In *Khasi* community, woman and man dance together, and the woman adorns the crown in her family and clan; but in 'public festivals' she has to dance keeping her eyes downcast. A married woman is not permitted to partake in the dances. It is indicative of the lower status and self-esteem of woman in comparison to man. The presence of maidens inside the male circle while dancing with the family suggests that it is the natural duty of the male to protect a female. This sense of duty (to safeguard women) springs from the masculine ethos that considers women more as a commodity than as equal beings."

In *Karbi* tribe, women preside over the ritual of *shradha*, an act that marks the propitiation of the departed souls. Herein, the role of lady singer is very significant, for it is believed that it is she who would lead the departed soul to its real abode, the heaven.

Women conduct or preside over all the wedding rituals in *Hajaang* community. *Ayarask* women perform all wedding functions—right from the decoration of the wedding-*mandapa* to '*uruli*'. They even help perform *pheras* or the circumbulation ceremony of the bride and the groom.

Barai custom is prevalent among the Rabha community. *Barai* denotes *gotra*. This *gotra* is related to the mother's side. At the time of the family/property division, father's property passes to the son and that of the mother to the daughter. But the children adopt their mother's *gotra*.

In the *Apatani* community of Arunachal Pradesh, the elder son inherits father's property and daughter gets mother's jewellery.

Women enjoy considerable respect in *Mizo* community. If during *Jhum* a man happens to touch her 'Pochai'—the special clothes kept apart for this purpose by women even accidentally, he is severely punished. *Mizo* women also plough the fields. In case a woman begets an illegitimate child, the *Mizos* have a custom whereby the child is bestowed with the identity of its father if the woman in question makes his name public and the father named by the girl, pays a penalty of forty rupees.

It is a fact that *Adivasi* women are relatively more independent than their non-tribal counterparts. Along with men, they participate in feasts and dance, in social activities and festivities, and work with equal zeal both within and outside the domestic sphere. On the one side the tribal community proclaims: 'Life lies in mutual sharing of food; to eat alone is to be dead; the one who hoards shall die and the one who distributes shall live; Life is mutual give and take; and never berate one's roots or clan.' On the other hand male chauvinism has been deeply ingrained within this 'tribal patriarchy' since antiquity. Whether it involves the division of work, or man's attitude towards woman, everything is underlined by masculinist ego and sense of dominance. Some of the following sayings amply illustrate this fact:

1. Women and crabs have no *dharma* or ethics.
2. Let the women and dogs bark as they wish.
3. A woman's intelligence doesn't stretch beyond the village well.

4. A man should never intervene when two women quarrel.
5. A woman is replaceable like an old hedge.

L.T. Khiangte, citing an incident from the life of tribal poetess Hmuaki, narrates a painful tale of male ego. Hmuaki composed a variety of lively songs for all occasions. Her fellow villagers feared that she might compose every possible verse and that the new generation will be left with no possibility of composing any new song. So they decided to bury her alive and dug up a grave for her last rites. They started filling the pit, Phmuaki once again burst forth in a quaint dirge:

Young ones, Oh dear young lads
Just bury me here softly with due care

Citing many more tales of woe, Khiangte underlines the prevalence of violence on tribal women but at the same time foregrounds the fact that these women not only raised their voice against its perpetration but also protested against it with commensurate logic. The gallant *Adivasi* women have even taken up arms to protect their community/country in the times of crises. Women from Jharkhand, namely Miko, Maki, Thigi, Sngi Dai, Kali Dai, Champi, Sali, Lembu, and the wives of Dunka Munda, Majhia Munda and Bankar Munda fought in the *Santal Hool,* Birsa *Ulgullan, Tana Bhagat* Movement and they had also participated in the struggle of Rohtasgarh, and had breathed their last only after killing their enemies. Among *Mizo* martyrs, Khiangte mentions Hmuaki, Ropuiliani, Darpawngi, Laltheri, Lianchhiari and Saikuti—they were not only fighters but also intellectuals. Jharkhand also boasts of many such brave women. They not only drove away the enemy but also defended their state and society. They did not belong to the royal family but were ordinary women.

When Mizo poetess Laltheri fell in love with a commoner, Chalthanga, her brothers beheaded him. Laltheri started crying aloud outside the chief's house. She tore off her clothes and threw away all her lovely beads and lay down naked in the courtyard, without wearing any clothes and necklaces.

Responding to the request of her mother with full conviction, she complained:

Mother, I shall not wear my clothes
As my lover lies cold and dead deep down

She blamed her parents for their wrongful deeds of killing her lover against her will:

How thoughtless are you, mother and father
Posting the head of Chalthanga in our courtyard

All these verses remind us of Shelley's statement, "The freedom of women produces the poetry of sexual love". Love became a religion, idols of whose worship were ever present. In Darpawngi's couplet, a sense of individuality and liberty is conspicuously present. She too was a born rebel.

Once during the reign of woman head of Zaadeng tribe, she went to Thentlang Darpawngi. There, her lambkin was snatched away by a middle-aged senior. In order to get her pet back, Darpawngi lodged a complaint against him. The villagers claimed that when placed in the middle, the lamb would naturally move over to her mother. As expected the lamb came to Darpawngi goat and began suckling it. But despite this the village handed over the lamb to that middle aged man. Darpawngi raised her voce against his injustice in her couplet, thus:

You the chief of Zaadeng, who claims to be just
I won't ever believe that the people live in peace in your village

Consequently, harassed by the village-head, she decided to leave for another village, saying:

I will definitely leave this village
That does not dispense justice under its rule

The foregoing discussion demonstrates that Adivasi women have fought injustice for centuries, and this struggle continues. A lot more can be told about the still untold plight of the *Adivasi* women, but they themselves have begun telling about it now. Though the civil society is awakening and raising its voice against discrimination, but for this to materialize the active cooperation of the state and society-as-a-whole is a must.

6

Problems of Women-Labourers in Mining and Tribal Areas and Their Solution

Even today, especially in mines and tribal areas, woman happens to be the cheapest but most useful commodity, on the scale of labour. It is true that since the nationalization of coal mines, a woman has been given wage parity with man, but this parity has cost her dearly. Apart from snatching her job away, it has also made her vulnerable to various kinds of exploitation. The problems that women face in nationalized collieries are different from the ones they face in non-government sector. But sexual harassment is a problem that cuts across industries, public and private, and regions and afflicts every woman-labourer (known as a *Kamin* or *Bojhari* in the coal belt in the Chhotanagpur now Jharkhand *Adivasi* belt) equally.

There is an intimate link between the agricultural field and the mine; the destruction of agricultural field/land leads to the creation of a mine. As more number of women than men are engaged in agriculture in the *Adivasi* belt, the crisis that they face in life is accordingly, proportionate to the spread of mines, dams and other developmental schemes in the region. There is almost no scheme for rehabilitation in this region, and whatever little employment opportunities come by in the wake of bitter struggle by these people, are exclusively apportioned to men. Women's employment has been banned in collieries. Though both men and women of this region work equally hard. Infect women work harder, still it is a man who is the focus of all rehabilitation schemes. Though in Jharkhand some of the land leases do exist in the name of women.

For the sake of convenience the problems that women face in the region under discussion are divided under three heads. However, the problems that are common to all women have been put together under a separate head. These categories include:

1. Problems of *Kamins* employed in collieries:
   (a) Problem of *Kamins* employed in Non-government collieries,
   (b) Problem of *Kamins* employed in Government collieries.
2. Problems faced by female agricultural labour due to the spread of mines and dams.
3. Problems faced by female labour in tribal belt and in rural areas.

Collieries are the biggest employer of *Kamins*, after agriculture sector. Apart from colliers women labour force also exist in large number in manganese, lime, fire clay, mica and copper mines and in stone quarries. Firstly, because of the compulsion to work on a wage lower than that of the male due to abundant availability of cheap labour, secondly, women's capacity and habit of working more diligently and for longer hours than men, the *Adivasi kamins* have been employed in large number in mines. However, with increasing mechanization, women's re-employment in collieries has been banned.

Apart from the usual domestic chores, the woman labourer also performs the following 'duties' as a matter of routine:

1. She hauls up the clay, stone and material (*i.e.*, coal, fire clay, stone etc.) that *malkattas*, or coal-cutter mine and carries it in baskets to a fixed place;
2. Loads the material in trucks;
3. Hauls up clày in trucks;
4. Breaks stones;

5. Chops *shrubs* trees for firewood and carries it on her head to the market;
6. Gathers *mahua;*
7. Gathers *tendoo* leaves, sorts them and ties them into bundles and supplies the material to contractors for making Beedies;
8. Gathers *saal* seeds and flowers;
9. Rolls *beedies;*
10. Vends vegetables;
11. Helps in harvesting, hoeing and sowing in the fields. Except for ploughing of fields, all other agricultural chores are done by a woman in the *Adivasi* belt;
12. Except for thatching the roof, which is considered as an exclusively male task, all other construction tasks, such as raising the walls, preparing mud mortar, arranging construction material, fetching thatch material and hauling it on to the roof etc., are carried out by females;
13. Ferments *mahua* for extracting liquor, prepares *hadia* (rice beer) etc. These tasks are primarily done by a woman; man only fills liquor in canisters and takes them to the market for selling. In most of the places, however, women also undertake these tasks. They carry the liquor to markets in *ghailas, i.e.* earthen pots.
14. Works in brick-kilns. Except for tasks prohibited by tradition, the tribal women are more efficient workers than their non-tribal counterparts in all other jobs. In fact all tasks—whether small or big—are given to women.

As compared to non-tribal woman, a tribal woman is more empowered and independent, socially and economically. She is free to spend her earnings herself. As a matter of fact, she faces greater exploitation at the hand of the non-tribal society.

Problems of *Kamins* Employed in Mines

Most of the women work in collieries. They work here in pairs or in *dangal* (gangs), that is, they work collectively by pairing with their husbands, brothers, and fathers or by aligning with a group of workers. As such if a woman lives alone or is separated from the family, or if she happens to be weak, indisposed or old, she has to face lots of problems. The collieries, both in public and private sectors that practise manual coal cutting, the labourers are employed on 'piece-rate' bases, and the salary they get is proportionate to the work done by them during the specified period. A woman, if she happens to be young, has to live either as someone's keep or has to keep the *munshi* satisfied, or has to plead with the head of the group, or has to leave a portion of her earnings with the gang *(dangal)*. Usually women work in *dangals*, or if married, work by pairing with their husbands. At places the family constitutes itself into a *dangal* and works together.

The second problem that women face identically in both public and private sector collieries is that of the absence of child-care centres for the children of working mothers. Consequently, the practice of leaving the child in the care of older children above mines or to lull it into sleep in the open on rocks still prevails. Even the permission to breast feed the child is dependent on the *munshi*. The *munshi* has to be given a bribe of a rupee or two every week for securing permission to breast-feed the child or to ensure that there is no wage cut due to occasional delays for duty. The private collieries don't even provide rest-shelters. Even in government collieries there are only a few shelters and that too in bad shape. In the Kuju region of CCL, while loading wagons at '*siding*' or site, it is usual for women labourers to make their babies sleep in the shade of the wagons. Most of the women employed for wagon loading have either been removed from jobs under 'golden handshake-scheme', or have been forced to seek voluntary retirement.

There is no provision for childcare from government. Whatever provisions exist are either on papers or are almost negligible. Coupled with these is the problem of maternity leave. Women keep on working till ten days before the delivery is due or till the commencement of labour pain. There is no provision of maternity benefits or leave in private collieries. In those collieries where the labour force is not organised, the woman keeps working till the time of delivery or the onset of labour pains. The number of dispensaries in collieries is not only inadequate; these don't even have enough lady-doctors or nurses. The managements are least bothered about extending the facility of maternity leave or providing pregnant workers with the facility of regular medical checkups. It is only after great difficulty and on 'asking/pleading' that the women are able to get advance for maternity leave, and here too the share of the *munshi* or office *babus* is fixed. Many a times this money is released/paid only after a year.

Even the husband—fearing a cut in earning—is not in favour of this leave. And wherever the woman works alone (in government collieries), and the husband is without work, it becomes all the more difficult for the woman to avail herself of the leave. Because of the scarcity of money even when she is working, she continues working well beyond the onset of labour pains—as it is neither within her control nor certain for how long she will have to sit idle after delivery. Though she gets her share from the *dangal* during the period of leave, the work being piece-rated, she would get more money only if she continued working. That's why she doesn't prefer to sit home on leave.

Her difficulties are compounded when her health aggravates during delivery. If she is not able to rejoin her duty after availing herself of maternity leave, initially her half and subsequently full salary is deducted. The maternity leave is for 45 days, three weeks before and three weeks after the delivery. If due to illness she has to go on leave much before this week pre-maternity period, she is left with only two-week after the delivery for recovery. Left with no leave-with-pay and being absent from duty she is paid no salary. Alternately, her absence is adjusted against sick or annual leave, if pending which invariably leads to cut in her income.

Yet another acute problem that women workers in collieries face is that of retrenchment. Even otherwise no dignity is attached to labour in India. However, with the recent increase of wages and job security in collieries the 'haves' have started eyeing even these jobs. The managements, in connivance with trade unions, have started phasing out women labourers from service in a systematic manner. This scheme came into force for the first time during the Emergency rule in 1976, under which a woman of any age, but with maximum limit of 57 (*i.e.*, with three years of job still left), could nominate her son, husband or husband's younger brother or any other person and seek voluntary retirement. The provident fund number of the woman is allotted to the person nominated by her. As a result in place of her son or husband, the outsider belonging to white collared class started buying these jobs in a large number initially by paying an amount ranging from 2000 to 10,000 rupees. This amount became 50,000 to 1,00,000 per job by 1982. Only a small portion of this amount reaches the concerned woman, most of it is distributed among the management officers, union leaders or the middlemen who initially ensnare this woman or at times, it is disbursed even among the sons and husband of the woman. White collared class has begun grabbing these jobs by producing false marriage certificates (from the court) of others, by declaring themselves as husbands of such women or daughters of these women before the magistrate. At times they actually married them. That's why today it is a common sight in collieries to come across Jha ji, Mishra ji, Dube ji, Upadhayaye ji, Singh ji, Sahu ji, or Mahato ji, *i.e.* all higher castes people. Have grabbed jobs in the garb of this voluntary retirement. Actually their so called father's or father-in-law's name happened to be Majhi, Munda, Uraon, Bhuian or Ganjhu. Though this scheme covers men of all castes but their too by and large it was Tribal, Dalits or women whose jobs were sold or purchased. This policy was, however, made more liberal for women; men could only exchange their jobs either with sons or son-in-laws.

Occasionally a white collared man does marry a maiden, divorcee or deserted woman, but as soon as he gets the job, or the female becomes pregnant, he leaves her, for he doesn't want this woman or her child to inherit his property. In the coalfields, one can see such women knocking at the doors of management and union leaders for lodging complaints. But their sexual exploitation continues unabated. It was only after the villagers, led by our union, filed a case in the Supreme Court, that this scheme was terminated by CCL. But this practice still persists covertly in the guise of ill health, though there has been one conspicuous change. Now it is either the son or the son-in-law only, who can force his mother/mother-in-law into illness to surrender her job to him. Even among women the tendency to sit idle after transferring the job to son/son-in-law is on the rise. But when they have to pay for it later they start complaining about their sons/sons-in-law—"I have been thrown out of home; he doesn't provide for me food and shelter now." In order to get a job under clause 9.4.2, *i.e.* after death of the worker the incidents of son/son-in-law killing even his ill parents or parents-in-law have become common. In order to arrange a daughter's marriage, the gifting of employment-card of either the mother or the father to the bridegroom during *Tilak* ceremony has become a routine. Article 9.4.3, which guarantees employment under NCWA-V also comes in handy in scouting for a groom. Article 9.4.3 means right to employment in case of illness, and 9.4.2 means right to be employed as dependant of the deceased. Recently, under the Voluntary Retirement Policy, 2000 women have been eased out of jobs in CLL alone. These voluntary schemes provide management with the tool to exploit women twice over. First, the management encourages a woman to seek voluntary retirement with promise of service to their sons/sons-in-law. On the receipt of application to this effect, she is made to undergo a fake medical examination wherein she is declared unfit, and is rested from work or in other words, she is stopped from marking her attendance. Thereafter her dependent is interviewed, and if found 'fit'/suitable, is given the promised appointment letter. After this he is asked to undergo medical examination and his police verification is done so as to verify the validity of his claim as son/son-in-law of the woman in question, a procedure that should have been completed simultaneously with the filing of application by that woman. At times the whole process takes one to two years to complete, before the son or the son-in-law can actually get the job. However, if in police verification, the claim of the dependant is proved to be false or otherwise, the woman cannot get her job back. If she demands her job back, the Coal India management offers her a fresh job which means that she loses on her gratuity and Provident Fund etc. We had suggested that whether it is Article 9.4.3 or special Voluntary Retirement Scheme, till the process of the nominee's verification is not complete, the woman should not be forced to step down from her job—this will automatically safeguard both her salary and her job. Otherwise this procedure should be completed within a time-frame of one week.

There is no provision to discuss women's problems exclusively. The facilities extended to males are supposed to cover their difficulties too. The shoes provided in the collieries furnish an apt example in this regard. Women are given heavy shoes that are actually meant for men. Women can't wear these. If they are supplied with 'right' shoes, these are either of wrong size or are in short supply. So far none has cared to get shoes specifically made for women. Given the Indian conditions, these shoes are a must. Though there has been an agreement between the management and trade unions to pass on the recommendation to this effect to the department of Mining and Security, the attitude of the department, however, remains indifferent.

Problems faced by Female Agricultural Labour due to the Spread of Mines

Large-scale acquisition of land for nationalised collieries and other public and private sector mines has created a huge class of unemployed women labourers. These women are faced with a plethora of intractable problems in comparison to men. In the succeeding paragraphs an attempt is being made to discuss some of the problems that women face due to the spread of mines.

Neither the companies nor the government has taken any concrete initiative for the implementation of rehabilitation schemes. And whatever resettlement scheme is being worked out, whether in the form of employment, or in the form of allotting land in place of land, or in the form of monetary compensation, women find no mention in it. A woman without a male heir cannot get job in collieries if her land is acquired. She can get a job only if she is a widow or if she does not have any earning male member in the family. Though a woman works as hard as any man, in the event of the acquisition of her land, she has no claim to the job and no share in the compensation. And if the government allots land, it is registered in the name of a male. Even otherwise an *Adivasi* woman has no right to property under the tribal community laws. She has the right to live with her parents if she is unmarried, or a widow, or is deserted by her husband, but has no right to property. In such a situation *Adivasi* males usually moves out of the region to big cities like Kolkata, Ranchi, Jamshedpur, and Patna or other states in search of livelihood. There they work as rickshaw pullers, or farm or brick-kiln labour or as workers in tea-estates in Assam etc. The women can be seen working in forests or on dams and roads as seasonal labour. After we had filed a case for rehabilitation and job (with a provision for women's share in the same) on behalf of the uprooted/dislocated people in the Supreme Court in 1980-81, the Court had given directions to include women's claim for job in the context of the Gobindpuri Project.

In areas with no mines or other industries, the men from *Dalit* or *Adivasi* community generally migrate to cities in search of jobs. Women along with their children tend to their homes all alone for nine months a year. Most of them survive either by selling firewood, or by doing the above listed jobs. The men return only in the rainy season for agriculture. The situation is a bit different in *Adivasi* areas. There the *Adivasi* couples, either on their own accord or through middlemen, move away in large numbers to far off states in search of employment. In contrast, the exclusive groups and groups of women (the only man who accompanies them generally looks after their working tools and kitchen utensils) from Chaibasa or Santal Pargana move out for loading and unloading trucks. Before nationalisation of collieries, it was mainly women who would do the loading and unloading job. Even now, in opencast mines and on the surface, this task is mostly performed by women.

In industrial areas, it is either the sons or the husband, who takes away a woman's earnings to spend it mostly on hooch or gambling. The women are thus bereft of any economic independence despite working hard for a week. This convention of handing over the woman's earning to her husband also persists in nationalised mines. We have continuously tried to resist this practice and have succeeded in getting a provision made whereby the working woman would receive her wage in person directly. But sometimes the women themselves authorize their men to collect their salary. Perhaps they do so out of fear or laziness. *Adivasi* women generally collect their wages themselves, for they are in the habit of working alone, separately from their men and also because their society sanctions their moving out alone for job. They work with their partners as equals not as slaves.

Women greengrocers have to travel a distance ranging from two to ten miles to reach the *haat* or the city to sell their vegetables; it is only after travelling such a distance that they are able to earn some money. The women who gather *mahua* generally fall prey to exploitation. The wood gathering women too find themselves in a similar situation. The women are victimized both by the owners of *mahua* trees, forest guards and the police. More often than not the people with muscle and money power from the surrounding areas lay illegal claim on *mahua* trees, though at times they might have actually bought these trees in auction. Anyway, for thirteen baskets of *mahua* collected, the tribal woman use to get only one; the rest are grabbed by the owner. It was later by our esitation that the rate improved and it became one basket out of three. These women barter away their *mahua* for salt, oil and other households and field items. They cook *mahua* and use it as food. They also extract liquor from it and oil from its seeds and sell it in the market. All this is a part of their economic structure. Tribal women are thought to be more efficient than their men folk in making and carrying bricks in brick kilns. That's why the *Adivasi* women from Santal Pargana and Chhotanagpur of Jharkhand are supplied by middle men to brick kilns around Patna and to different corners of Bihar/Bengal or to other places in India, on very meagre wages. They are forced to work there for 12 hours a day. One can find *Adivasi*-women of this region working in agricultural fields in far off states like Punjab,

Haryana and Andhra Pradesh. A large number of these women are also being taken to tea-gardens. In Andaman the *Adivasi*-couples who were taken there years ago from places like Ranchi, Hazaribagh and Santal Pargana, have established their own colonies. They were initially kept near the areas where there were cannibals tribes, *i.e.* cannibals were living. These cannibals continue to attack them stealthily. These people have been settled in places where even during the day, one cannot go without police escort. *Adivasi* women, however, don't fear working in adverse situations.

The most pernicious laws for tribal women happen to be those which have ostensibly been enacted to safeguard them. While putting restraints on the owners/masters, these laws are meant to extend certain facilities to these women. In the first section there is a prohibition on putting women on night shifts and a ban on employing them in underground mines. In the second section there is a provision for welfare laws such as (1) maternity leave, (2) wage parity with men, (3) rest shelters at the work place, and (4) care centres/crèche for the children of working women etc.

The prohibition on work during night shifts and in underground mines act as the biggest obstacle in women's employment, and since this rule is followed in the nationalised collieries; it has not only put a stop to the re-employment of women, it has also paved a well thought out way for their retrenchment. The provisions of maternity leave and wage parity also discourage profiteers from employing women. It has been observed that in private collieries where the management can afford to ignore these rules, more women than men are employed in the mines.

Woman's Daily Routine in Tribal Areas

A tribal woman typically follows the following daily routine— She gets up in the morning and cleans the house, mops the floor and plasters the hearth, fires the hearth, fetches water from far off springs, rivers or deep wells, or other sources. Many a time it takes hours for her to fill a pitcher or *ghaila* with water using a bowl. Cooking is also her responsibility. In the meanwhile a man, except brushing his teeth, does nothing. She eats only after having served food to her husband, children and the elderly. To scrub utensils is a rule with her. If there are milch animals like cows etc., in the house, then it is also her duty to look after them. Having finished the household chores she either accompanies her husband in search of a job or accompanies him to the forest to chop firewood. Both chop the wood together, and then the woman carries the wood on her head to the market. After this the woman has to cook the meal for the night. Sleeping after her husband as he has gone to sleep and waking up before him is a part of her daily routine.

Primitive Malpractices and Industrial Growth

1. Witch Custom

The women of *Ho* tribe that inhabit the thick forests of southern Chhotanagpur now in Jharkhand and whom industrialization hasn't impacted so far, are still trapped in the web of witchery and evil spirits. However, in no way are they inferior to men economically. Contrary to it, where industrial progress has slackened the hold of these evil customs and rituals, women are not only falling prey to decaying morals and sexual exploitation but also to half-baked middle-class mentality. Quite often men and women of this region tend to brand any woman a *dayan*, or a witch. In the wake of some incident/ accident in the village, a barren, or a widowed woman, an outspoken woman or a woman with a peculiar past, is considered responsible for the incident and proclaimed a *dayan*. She has to undergo both physical as well as economic punishment. Sometimes she is even beaten to death. She is forced even to eat excreta.

2. Woman as a Stake in Gambling

To use women as a wager in gambling is yet another evil practice that is prevalent in mines. I know of two such incidents.

They had taken place in Kedla, Jharkhand and Laio collieries respectively. In the latter the workers of Laio colliery having won a *Kamin* (working woman) of Jharkhand had taken her away. We had to intervene to secure her freedom. In the former, a worker of Kedla colliery lost his wife. When the 'lost' woman refused to go along with her winner, her husband sliced her nose with a knife. The fact of the matter is that these women though earning their livelihood themselves, have not become self-dependant, hence cannot take a decision on their own. They are still considered to be the property of the husband or the family. The *Adivasi* women, however, are not as dependant as non-tribal women are. The physical relations among tribal people are simple and straightforward. Force is not used. Mutual liking, what in literature or civil society may be called as love, is the main basis of relationship. It may be called as mutual attraction (in the language of Nature). No irrational or illogical prohibitions exist among these people. Mistaking this uninhibited tendency of theirs as wantonness, the non-tribal outsiders, under false promises or greed, tempt the tribal women to elope with them. Because of this unbecoming conduct of the outsiders a bitter schism, verging on hatred, has been created between tribal and non-tribal people.

The women in this region are also faced with the problem of polygamy. A man is free to marry a number of times. Though a woman is free to move out with another man, but at a time she cannot have more than one husband in these areas (though in Himachal Pradesh a woman can have 4 to 5 husbands), while a man can have many wives simultaneously (though there is a law to have one wife only). However, by paying a penalty, the man and woman in this region can easily take on a new wife or a husband. After community feast and consultations, the new husband or wife is granted legitimacy. Yet another interesting custom that is worth taking note of exists in this region. If a woman leaves her husband or if the husband dies, the woman is free to take her children along with her. The new man has to take the responsibility of nurturing these children, in other words the notion of step-mother and stepfather forms an integral part of this culture. The stepfather, however, is generally kind to these children. Step-mother is not a symbol of cruelty in these communities. Exceptions can however be found anywhere. On growing up, the son goes to his real father in his original village to take charge of his property. The marriage of the girl is the responsibility of the step father. Sometimes even the first or the real father comes forward to help. Dowry system does not exist among tribal communities. Here the groom's father gifts clothes and wedding expenses to the bride's father. There was no dowry system even among *Dalits* or 'backwards'. Now, however, this evil practice has taken root even among them; both the price and status of boys in jobs have been on the increase, especially after the nationalization of mines. Since there is lots of income in collieries, not only dowry but the practice of second marriage is also on the rise.

The *Saan* Custom of Mizoram

The problems like this are infinite, but here I have tried to sketch some of the more obvious ones only. I had been to Mizoram, Manipur and Assam recently. The women there are relatively more independent. In Mizoram, after marriage, the woman instead of adopting the surname of her husband would retain the genealogy of her parents. However, now-a-days, because of increasing influence of property and affluence, she too has started adopting the surname of her husband. Here, under the custom of *saan, i.e.* on payment of rupees forty as penalty, the child born before or outside marriage could get the name of his father. But this custom does not exist in other tribes of the country, and fearing ignominy, many women kill such children at birth. In Mizoram women get wages equal to that of men. Every woman weaves her clothes herself on looms there. In the choice of clothes they are more independent and affluent compared to women of elsewhere. In Assam, there is a provision of latrines for women at home even in rural areas. In contrast, for the women of Chhotanagpur and Santal Pargana and in other villages—barring government quarters and residences—this facility is nonexistent. There is no provision for bathrooms, toilets, or potable water for women working in mines. As a result they face many difficulties. There are no public toilets or bathrooms in mines and industrial institutions, though they exist in plans or on papers. At times they crumble before they are even used as *malkattas* or coal-cutters rarely use them.

Despite all semblance of economic self-dependence, if the women of this country, or for that matter of the whole world, do not unite and take effective steps to safeguard their interests, they will not be able to achieve the independence of their hearts' desire; and this civilization will keep on treading them under its feet, instead of empowering and emancipating them. The solution to this problem calls for a full-fledged research in this area.

In this region, or for that matter in every village, the problems of women keep on changing and increasing with each new situation. I have already shed light on some of the major problems. I now offer suggestions to solve some of these problems:

Public Security

Some of the aforementioned problems spring from the very laws ostensibly enacted to guarantee security, welfare and minimum wages to women. Some of the suggestions to overcome difficulties arising from these can be put as—(i) Maternity Leave, (ii) Creche and Care Centres for Children of these women, and (iii) the provision for Public Insurance. The implementation of these facilities still depends on the management and the owners, for it is they who are supposed to spend for/on these facilities. I think that the government should, at its own expenditure, start an institution of 'public security' and bring under its ambit the female workers engaged in industries, tea estates, and agriculture throughout the country. The government can, of course, recover a certain percentage of the expenditure incurred on this scheme from private managements, public sector and other institutions. It will ensure that private owners don't fight shy of employing women, or evade their problems. This fund should be levied on every management as a 'special cess,' irrespective of the fact that it does or doesn't employ women. This will make the whole industry responsible and contribute to the welfare of women labourers employed in various fields.

I had participated in the 11th conference of AICFTU held in Mexico in 1975. Under its aegis in a seminar at Koriabanca the women participants had made the above mentioned proposal.

(A) Maternity Leave

Elsewhere in the world there has been demand for granting maternity leave to the husband along with his wife. This will have double benefit—one, maternity leave won't affect woman's employment, and, two, the man will be by his woman's side during this period and, more importantly, spend time in the care of the child. This rule is in force in many countries. It will also reinforce the belief that child care is the responsibility of both the parents and not that of the mother alone.

(B) Rules Regarding Night Shift and Underground Scheme

The rules prohibiting women from working in night shifts and in underground mines have adversely affected women's employment, especially in collieries. In Mexico, women had successfully struggled to put a stop to law that has the practice of night shifts for women workers. Their argument was that working in night shift for women is not good hence it is not good for any human being also, *i.e.* for men also. In developing countries, the capitalist class uses this argument as a pretext to prohibit women only from getting jobs. In my opinion women should also be employed even for the third shift. If no consensus is reached on this, then they should be allowed to work atleast in second shift, so that the condition of those families—where the economic situation remains bleak, despite both men and women working simultaneously—could be ameliorated. On the one hand, working in second shift will improve their economic condition, and on the other, it would ensure regular work. In essential services too, a provision should be made for the third shift. It will help increase women's employment in those jobs that ensure regular income. That will also boost their economic freedom. I had made these proposals in the aforementioned conference in Mexico.

(C) Mine Norms

It is true that the provision of employing women in mines is detrimental within the social situation obtaining in the country, nay the world over; for, apart from converting women into a tool of sexual exploitation, it also harms their daily lives. But in such a situation the government should fix the ratio of women's employment in mines, and increase the quantum of women's employment for surface job in the first shift. Before nationalisation, the number of women employees in mines was quite big. If the quota for women is fixed, managements will not be able to remove them. Loading trucks, hauling clay/mud, cleaning the depots, making clay-balls and extracting or hauling coal or other minerals from quarries, all these tasks can be performed within the rules; hence the government should bring in an enactment to put a stop to the substitution of women by men or machines in these jobs. More women should be employed in normal shifts. Now-a-days the managements, especially in collieries, are bent on bringing in machines in place of women. This tendency needs to be curbed. The management should bring in employment friendly schemes; in case the machines are brought in, they should absorb the employees by training them for machines. Women should also be given technical training. They should also be employed in non-traditional jobs.

(D) Voluntary Retirement Scheme

Women are being retrenched systematically under a well thought out plan. Though the farm hands, men and women of Mandu, under my leadership had filed a case in the Supreme Court and secured a stay order against this scheme that had forced the management to stop this practice, yet the authorities kept open the doors for retrenchment of women in the garb of Article 9.4.3, discussed earlier. Some trade unions to serve their own vested interests are supporting the hereditary employment scheme. This way they are actually ostensibly helping in systematic retrenchment of women. Government should scrap this provision, and if this scheme needs to be continued for reasons of age or illness, then it should be accompanied by a rider that the retired women would be replaced in job by an equal number of other women. Only thus the exploitation of women can be stopped, and their jobs protected. In collieries, this matter needs to be given special attention.

The Question of Night Shifts for Women

This is a contentious one. Since this issue is intimately related with the question of women's employment, it calls for a thorough debate before any decision on it could be arrived at. As per mining security and factory rules, night shift duties are prohibited for women; whereas in service sector—offices, aeroplanes, hotels and many other fields—night shifts for women is a regular practice. In 1975, when as a representative of INTUC, I had gone to participate in an International Seminar of ICFTU. There the women, after a prolonged struggle, had succeeded in making their governments acquiesce to this demand of night shifts for women. Their argument was that the existence of this law not only denied women the night shifts and restricted their job options, but also at the same time this very law was employed as a pretext by the management to phase out women at the time of retrenchment. They had also argued that if night shift was harmful for women, then it was equally so for men. And if women cannot be entitled to work during night shifts, so be it with men; this would help create equal job opportunities for both.

In thickly populated countries, like India, this issue needs to be debated thoroughly, for it is here that the rights and employment opportunities if women are curtailed in the name of rules.

Yet another argument that is advanced in the context of countries like India and Pakistan postulates that since in these countries women are faced with greater social restraints than women in the West, their employment in nightshirts will expose them to increased risk of sexual exploitation, and hence they should not be allowed to work during these shifts. Most of the labour unions think this way. Most of the women organisations themselves resist the idea of night shifts without giving it a practical thought; their resistance at times is an ironic echo of the protest some of them had carried out against harsh family planning measures in the name of infringement on women's rights, thus sabotaging the implementation of these laws. Likewise the environmentalists raise the issue of environment leading to the closure of factories, industries and quarries without bothering about the plight of workers; they seldom agitate for reforms and alternative options within the existing scenario. As a result, fearing retrenchment, the labour/workers turn against these movements. It is important to keep in mind the practical issues while framing laws/rules for women.

This issue had come before us after the nationalization of collieries. Before it, the number of women working in collieries was almost equal to that of men and they would even work at night loading coal in wagons or trucks. They would also work along coal cutters in mines till nine or ten at night. In Hesagarh coalfields in Kuju of Mandu subdivision of Hazaribagh district, they used to work even in underground mines. Post nationalization, due to security norms they were not only stopped from working in underground mines, but were also stopped from loading trucks at night, in the entire Kuju region that had six large collieries, thus paving way for their retrenchment. The rationale of the management was that it being against the security norms, women could not be employed in night shifts and that since they had no new job or new project starting soon, they could not provide alternative jobs to them. The existence of surplus labour that had eventuated retrenchment of women first was yet another rationale advanced by the management. I, representing my union, had put a proposal that till new projects come into being and create job opportunities for women, the permission allowing women to work till ten at night may be sought from the department of mining security, and the day shift that goes till six in the evening may be rescheduled from six in the morning to two in the afternoon as a continuous shift and from two in the afternoon to ten in the night—so that women may continue with their jobs. Otherwise, the provision may be made for these women to work in other mines. To retrench a woman simply for the reason of her being a woman was not acceptable to us. The workers also rallied behind us and we succeeded in getting them to work till 10 pm. The men cooperated because most of those who worked there worked in twos—husband and wife, brother and sister, mother and son, daughter and father-in-law, or some other relation. The second reason for this success probably lay in my being a woman, who despite the presence of male cadre in the union enjoyed the right to take decision or give direction. Inverting every anti-woman norm I began that fight for justice, knowing full well that within the context of contemporary laws we were vulnerable.

From us, who talk of equality and seek job parity, this issue demands a commitment: let us shed our 'touch-me-not' image, and as competent women, adapt ourselves for every task and make ourselves capable of taking risks. And I can say this on the basis of my own experiences that this 'touch-me-not-complex' is typically middle class syndrome. It does not exist in lower castes or *Dalit* women. Yes, being as they are illiterate and unorganised, they fall prey to exploitation, especially sexual-exploitation. But even those women—be they from middle class or *Dalits*—who don't work outside are also vulnerable to this kind of exploitation, and they are in fact being exploited. Hence to reduce employment opportunity for women, or to affect their retrenchment, by linking the time or place of work to their vulnerability to sexual exploitation is totally unjustified and a mere pretence. **It is because of male chauvinism that a woman is exploited, be she a *Sawarna* or a *Dalit*, high or low class. If a middle or high class woman can work as a telephone operator or a hotel receptionist, then**

why should these other women be denied employment by refusing them work in factories and mines at night? There should instead be a demand for and provision of night escort/ vehicle for women working at night. It is imperative to organise and educate (not make them merely literate), and to make them aware of their rights—so that they can immediately lodge a complaint against any kind of exploitation and get redressal.

3. *Mechanism for Equal Wage Implementation*

Though the laws exist for equal wages, yet the machinery that is supposed to implement these has neither the capability nor the requisite integrity. The people, who are supposed to get it implemented, employ double standards themselves. There should be a system of summary trials to immediately look into and set right any problem that a woman worker might face. It would be necessary to amend labour laws to effect this change. It is very difficult even for male workers, what to talk of female labour, to approach the tribunal, High/Supreme Court within the purview of present laws.

4. *Share of Women in House Allotment*

According to current norms if the husband has a house allotted in his name, his wife cannot get an independent house. According to me, woman should be treated as a separate unit and allotted an independent house.

5. *Provision for Proper Shoes*

In this region or in rural India, women generally do not wear shoes. In collieries women are generally given the shoes meant for men, whereas they, considering the ground reality, should get lighter shoes.

6. *Women Officers*

It is important to employ some women officers so as to ensure efficient administration in mines, where women labourers work. This will ensure speedy redressal of women's complaints. Wages should be given directly to women. Though there exists a common norm that provides for handing over the wages to the person himself/herself, yet this law is generally violated in case of women. So wherever this question of paying wages to women directly is concerned there should be a legal provision for penalizing the management if it violates the provision. It will instill fear of law in management and would ensure that it pays wages directly to women workers and not hand it over to their husbands, who might splurge it on liquor or in gambling.

Suggestions for the Welfare of Women Labourers

The following are meant to safeguard the interests of women labourers and those women in tribal areas who move out of their houses to other states in search of jobs.

1. Food for Work

The schemes like "Food for Work" should be implemented extensively in rural areas so that people don't leave their villages and the villages may develop. Bihar was the biggest beneficiary of this scheme since its inception in 1978-79. Because of this scheme the village workers, especially women were freed from the stronghold of big landlords who would force them to drudge for a kilogram of grain or a quarter kilogram of *sattu*. Despite all sort of pilferage, women would still manage to get two to two and a half kilograms of grain—a lot more than what she would get from a *zamindar*—out of the stipulated four kilograms under food for work scheme. Labourers won't move out of the village, if they get food/grains within the village itself. It would also help them realize the importance of collective bargaining. While handing over the documents of land to the landless, the government should give separate papers to women. This land would give them a base to withstand the exploiters.

2. *Women Squads to Check Exodus*

The government should deploy women squads at main railway stations so as to prevent—by establishing links with them—unnecessary and large scale exodus of women labourers to other states and to arrange for their employment at their own place or in their own states. Alternately these squads can keep a track of their whereabouts and also inform the authorities of the respective states about them. This will ensure their protection against potential exploitation. The name, address and identity of the person, who is taking them away, should also be registered. It must be made mandatory for the labour suppliers to obtain a licence, so as to prevent unethical and exploitative activities.

3. *Minimum Wage Guarantee for Self-Employed Women*

As far as women working in villages and forests, on roads, and fields, or engaged in selling of wood and vegetables, or in gathering and selling *mahua* and its seeds, *sal* and *kusum* flowers and *tendu* leaves are concerned, all these jobs are either temporary or fall under the category of self-employment. At many places, no minimum wage has been fixed for these jobs so far. And where they has been fixed, there neither the government has shown any inclination to implement them, nor is there any machinery or system in place for the purpose. In Bihar till 1975, a labourer engaged in forest work was paid only three rupees. After our union fought for it, the labour rate was raised to rupees five. When rural employment scheme was introduced, the rate was fixed at rupees 10.75, but even then a woman did not get more than rupees five and man not more than rupees seven. Now the wages have been increased but the labour seldom gets full wages. To ensure full payment the government should enact a law with a system of 'reward-and-punishment' for village-*panchayats* and should enforce it strictly; however, *panchayat* elections have not taken place in Jharkhand for years, say decades. It is also important to organize women in these villages. For this, women social activists will have to forsake fashionable social activities and actively participate in trade union movements.

Now-a-days a new method of self-employment has come in vogue. This involves loading of coal in trucks from depots adjacent to coal mines. There the drivers or owners of trucks pay to the labour directly through their *dangal*/gang leaders. A large number of women and children are employed in this activity. Depending on their organization, their labour-rates vary from 400, 600 or 1000 to 1200 rupees per truck. But whether it would be rupees 400 or 1200 or somewhere in-between, it depends on their capacity to struggle and organize; there is no government control over it. A class of self-proclaimed *munshis* who act as brokers between drivers and gang leaders has sprung up in this region. They take commission varying from rupees 100 to 200 from truck drivers and from labour separately. In case the labour originally contracted to load the truck, failed to show up, these brokers sell the loading rights to other labourers at half the original rate and in the process earn heavy commission. These brokers are generally unemployed *rangdaars* from the village. It was only in Rallygarha that we could get identity cards issued to labourers and where government *munshi* allots vehicles. Elsewhere exploitation continues. These unemployed *rangdaars* and *dalals* are the fallout of rampant unemployment, displacement from agriculture lands and the predominance of feudal tendencies.

4. *Categorization of Women's Domestic Chores as 'Work'*

One important point that I would like to underline categorically pertains to a tendency that refuses to treat the work undertaken by women in their own field as 'work' despite the fact that they always put in more labour in comparison to men in the fields. As they work in the field—be it that of their husband, son or father—like any ordinary worker, minimum labour/wage for their work should also be fixed. When men join to run a business in partnership, the value of each one's labour/share is worked out and claimed, and this is even reckoned in income/expenditure. Why is woman's share not accounted for then? Neither the government nor man considers her work as work. The irony is that even women refuse to consider their work as work despite the fact that their work is akin to that of a business partner or a shareholder. In Non-Aryan culture the word *Ardhangini* denoted a sharing-partner. Shiva considered Parvati as his *ardhangini*, a partner, and not as an *anugamini* or a follower like Aryan. The Aryan culture/civilization reduced *ardhagini* into a ritualistic concept and confined her within the four walls of the house, whereas among the non-Aryans, whom Aryans had reduced into slaves and *Dalits*, she still works with equal ease. She is not imprisoned within the four-walls like *Sawarna* women. She does is both within and outside the house. The situation of *Sawarna* women is pitiable. She is a washer-woman, a cook, a cleaner, a nurse, a breast feeder and a sexual object/lap doll, all rolled into one, or in other words, she has to enact all roles—of a wife, mother, daughter, sister and a keep—yet her drudgery is not even taken note of. What to speak of economic compensation, her work is not even categorized as 'work'. This happens because she is 'notionally' circumscribed within the definition of family. She is considered property and not a part of the house; hence it is not she but the family that has claim over whatever she earns or does. Whatever she does is considered to be a part of her routine, a way of life, or a mandatory condition for her being. When a woman, at the end of the day's drudgery, is asked, "What did you do?" her most probable answer would be, "nothing". Her domestic chores will have to be brought under the definition of 'work,' perhaps only then woman would be able to value her being or her identity. Unless she learns to value herself, man will not give her due recognition.

5. *Low Cost Canteens for Freedom from Domestic Drudgery*

In order to liberate women, who work both in houses and mines, from the endless drudgery of domesticity, the provision should be made to provide them with packed food/tiffin prepared commercially. There should be low cost canteen facilities available for them. These facilities should be provided by the management/government at the place of their work, so that these women can be spared from the task of cooking prior to or after the job.

6. Provision of Potable Water

If arrangement for potable water is made in villages, it will go a long way in lessening the burden of working women. If, along with its rural health projects, the government can arrange for *latha, chhavan* and firewood, especially for the women of Chhotanagpur region in Jharkhand, it would help them get rid of the exploitative nexus of state-machinery, and also give them economic independence.

7. Legal Counselling, Training and Help in Case of Sexual Abuse/Exploitation

To protect them from sexual exploitation, these women need to be organized. Besides legal justice they also need legal awareness and knowledge. For this the government and NGOs should conduct courses/classes from time to time. Literature in simple language should be published for them. Besides providing adult education, the management should also be made responsible for educating them about their rights. The arrangement for this should be made at the very place where these women work. The management should arrange weekly classes at their work place so that they are made aware of their rights. The adult education programme should also be started at mines and factories (during duty with pay) so that women can count their wages and put signatures on the receipt, and also calculate their wages and work accurately.

8. Training Women for Non-traditional Jobs

In addition to mining jobs they should also be trained as telephone operators, teachers, doctors, lawyers, air-hostesses, clerks, stenographers, and receptionists. They may also be given technical training required for working as electricians, fitters or as drivers and dozers-pump-dumper-drill-operators, conventionally non-traditional professional jobs. Women can perform such jobs efficiently, especially those living in tribal areas or working in mines. In Assam women even run such shops.

9. Equal Share for Women in Land Compensation

Probably due to the non-existence of laws granting equal share in property, the women in general and *Adivasi* women in particular, are not given equal share in the employment for the displaced. The government should take steps to ensure it. The compensation for the land acquired for mining, should not only be given to men but also to women equally, for they work not only as much as the men do, but in many cases even harder than them. The women from this area run the house by not only earning in tandem with men, but at times by working all alone.

In order to restore their lost freedom, *Adivasi* women will have to be given back their old sustenance structures like right to forest to bring *latha, firewood* and *thatching material*, the right over land, and the share in the village organization. Steps should also be taken to develop their handloom and cottages industry and provide facilities for marketing of goods thus manufactured. It is only then that *Adivasi* and Dalit women can be made self-reliant. In these areas handloom can be one of the good sources of income for these women, like it is for women of Mizoram, Manipur, Assam and other Northeast states. In Northeast states handloom is one of the important bases of women's autonomy. Here there is no difference in the wages of men and women.

For all the other problems to which I have drawn attention, the legal provisions are in place, but they have to be enforced strictly. The tradition of killing a woman by branding her a witch; the practice of polygamy, the habit of women battering after drinking—all these evils will be eradicated by social reforms and education, but by granting them right to their land the economic freedom for women can be ushered in immediately. The emphasis should also be on providing women with technical education. Management should reserve fixed quota for women in jobs that are available. Women can take maximum advantage from reservation in jobs. For this, provisions would have to be made for women's reservation through amendment in the Constitution.

(A modified version of the paper presented by the author at the seminar on "The Contribution of Women in Restructuring India", at IIC, Delhi, organized by Indian Development Council.)

Index